Celtic Baby Names

BOOKS BY JUDY SIERRA

Cinderella
Fantastic Theater
The House That Drac Built
Multicultural Folktales
Nursery Tales Around the World
Quests and Spells
Storytellers' Research Guide
Wiley and the Hairy Man

WITH BOB KAMINSKI

Multicultural Folktales
Twice Upon a Time
Children's Traditional Games

CELTIC BABY NAMES

*Traditional Names from
Ireland, Scotland, Wales, Brittany,
Cornwall & the Isle of Man*

JUDY SIERRA
PH.D.

folkprint
eugene, oregon

FOLKPRINT
Post Office Box 450
Eugene, OR 97440
(541) 683-9752

Copies of this book may be ordered from the publisher for $14.95 plus $3.00 shipping and handling. Inquire about foreign rates via e-mail to sierra@continet.com.

Manufactured in the United States of America

Cover design by Lyle Mayer

Initials by John D. Batten appeared in *Celtic Fairy Tales* (1892) and *More Celtic Fairy Tales* (1894) by Joseph Jacobs.

Library of Congress Cataloging-in-Publication Data:

Sierra, Judy.
    Celtic baby names : traditional names from Ireland, Scotland, Wales, Brittany, Cornwall, and the Isle of Man / Judy Sierra.
        p.   cm.
    Includes bibiliographical references (p.) and index.
    ISBN 0-9636089-5-9 (paper)
    1. Names, Personal--Celtic--Dictionaries.   I. Title.
CS2377.S48   1997
929'.4'4'0899162--dc21   96-52432
                                                                            CIP

CONTENTS

 his book is a guide to over 1200 personal names and nicknames from the six Celtic languages, along with a few from ancient Gaulish and British for good measure. Currently, four Celtic languages are spoken in Europe: Irish in Ireland, Gaelic in Scotland, Welsh in Wales, and Breton in Brittany. Cornish, which once flourished in the southwest corner England, and Manx, from the Isle of Man in the Irish Sea, ceased being community languages a century or more ago, but live on in the names of people and places, and in vital language revival movements.

Genuine Celtic names are of interest not only to parents, but to adults seeking meaningful and melodious names for themselves, and to authors looking for names for literary characters. Some Celtic names are attractive simply because of their pleasing spelling and sound. Many of them are tantalizingly close to English names, but with appealing twists, such as the Irish Dealla and Niall; Cornish Kelyn and Meryn; Breton Derrien and Yvona; Welsh Bryn and Ceri; Scottish Calum and Mirren; and Manx Kerron and Bree.

Some Celtic names can be traced back 2,000 years to a time when everyone understood their meanings, like the Welsh Auron, which means 'golden goddess', Teyrnon 'divine prince', and Meriel 'bright sea'. The Breton Gwencalon signifies 'shining heart' and the Irish Ríordan was 'a royal poet'. I have given the etymology of each name when it is known. Scholars disagree about the meaning of some names. I have chosen those I judge to be most reliable, though these are not always the most romantic or beautiful: the name Kennedy derives from the Old Irish for 'ugly head', while the Scottish name Cameron comes from Gaelic words meaning 'crooked nose'.

Celtic names are associated with queens and kings, heroines and heroes, saints and scholars. The spelling and pronunciation of names changed over time. The Old Irish royal name Conchobar became Conor, and the queenly Eithne became Enya. Other old Celtic names have recently been revived. Dylan, Welsh for 'ocean', was a sea-child in the *Mabinogi,* but a name seldom given babies until 1914 when schoolmaster Gwilym Thomas chose the name for a son who carried not only the name but the Celtic gift of poetry as well.

Common European Christian names were adopted and changed by the speakers of Celtic languages, and today these names provide charming alternatives to overused English ones. Parents can choose the Breton name Yannick instead of John, or Katell for Catherine; the Irish Liam or Welsh Gwilym for William; Cornish Daveth for David; Manx Moirrey instead of Mary; or the Scottish Gaelic Alasdair for Alexander.

Many Celtic names are associated with saints. Christianity was widely accepted among all levels of society in early Celtic Britain and Ireland, and it seems that every other religious person who lived from the 5th through the 7th century achieved sainthood. Most of these early saints were canonized by local custom rather than through official recognition by Rome. For parents who wish to follow the tradition of giving a child the name of the saint on whose feast day it was born, there is a calendar of saints' days on page 109.

This book is intended for parents and others who live outside the Celtic regions, and I have selected only those names I think will be most pleasing and interesting to English speakers. More names from each region can be located through the specialized books listed in the bibliography. The pronunciations included in this book approximate the way a modern speaker of the language with little or no regional accent would say the names. I leave it to the readers to decide how best to adapt these pronunciations, which in many cases will sound a bit odd to the English-attuned ear.

This book could not have been compiled without the work of the dedicated Celticists whose books are listed in the bibliography. I received invaluable assistance with Continental Celtic and Brythonic languages from Leslie Ellen Jones. Grateful thanks as well for advice and pronunciation to Mary Davis, Mairéad de Londra, Marion MacIsaac, Amy Hale and Gwennole Le Menn. The responsibility for any errors or misinterpretations of their excellent work is my own.

PRONUNCIATION GUIDE

a	as in	cat	h	as in	hot
ah	"	father	j	"	just
aw	"	all, box	k	"	cat
ay	"	say	l	"	lucky
e	"	met	m	"	mother
ee	"	meet	n	"	now
i	"	big	ng	"	sing
ii	"	bite	p	"	pat
o	"	not	r	"	rock
oh	"	note	s	"	saint, race
oi	"	toy, boil	sh	"	sharp
oo	"	boot	t	"	ton
ow	"	out	th	"	bath
uh	"	ago, but	*th*	"	bathe, father
b	"	box	v	"	very
ch	"	chop	w	"	west, quiet
d	"	dig	y	"	you, cute
f	"	fit	z	"	zoo, his
g	"	gate	zh	"	pleasure

Special sounds

lh   Welsh; place your tongue to make the sound of the letter *l* then breathe out a short, sharp breath.

rh   Welsh; place your tongue as for a Spanish *r*, then breathe out a short, sharp breath.

x   as in Scottish *loch* or German *ich;* a sound halfway between the *h* in 'oh, hey' and *k* in 'okay'.

CELTIC REALMS, CELTIC NAMES

n around 700 BC, in the Salzammergut region of what is now Austria, a group of people who were making a good living from the salt mines at Hallstatt took their first steps into the Iron Age. This technological revolution had an effect on their social life, as their art and material culture began to develop an idiosyncratic style that differed from that of other tribes around them. Their wealth increased, and their neighbors, who could recognize a good thing when they saw it, began to adopt their way of life and their language as well. By around 500 BC, this Celtic culture had spread throughout the Alps region and into central Europe. A new style of art, marked by curving lines and a surreal abstracted naturalism, became fashionable. La Tène culture, named after the town on Lake Neuchâtel in Switzerland where it was first investigated in the 19th century, marked the convergence of many influences into a Celtic way of life. The Celts were united partly by ties of blood and geography, but more importantly by a shared technology and a common language that facilitated the trade of goods and ideas. Their civilization spread throughout Europe not so much as the result of warfare and conquest, but rather of commerce. The people of Hallstatt traded salt, which was so important a commodity that before the invention of coinage it was the equivalent of money. Later, the Celts became renowned for their metal work, a fact reflected in the importance of the blacksmith in Celtic mythology.

No one knows exactly why the Celts turned their attention from trading to raiding around the 4th century BC. It seems likely that their improving standard of living led to a rise in population, and their land couldn't support the increasing burden. Unfortunately, nearby regions were already populated by Etruscans, Romans, Greeks and others who didn't feel like sharing their space, so the Celts tried to take it by force. In 390 BC, a Celtic army commanded by a chief named Brennus raided the city of Rome; in 279 BC, another Celtic army under another chief named Brennus sacked the Greek temple at Delphi. Elsewhere, whole tribes seem to have just picked up and wandered around until they found a niche where they could fit in, and then stayed there.

By 200 BC, Celtic civilization had reached the outer limits of its expansion, from Galicia in Spain to Galatia in Turkey, all of France (called Gaul by the Romans), and the islands of Britain and Ireland. Celtic tribes fought amongst themselves and with their neighbors, but apparently ceased their long-distance raiding, though their warriors, both men and women, still inspired the awe of the Greeks and Romans. The next two centuries saw the expansion, in turn, of Rome. Across western Europe, Celtic languages were replaced by Latin. Only on the periphery of the Empire—in Britain and the unconquered lands of Ireland and Scotland—did the Celtic culture and languages prevail.

Celtic languages

Celtic languages are part of the Indo-European language family and are related to nearly all the other languages of Europe. Celtic is the name of a group of similar languages, and it is also the name of the ancestor of all the Celtic languages, which was once spoken in central Europe. Linguists have reconstructed some of the vocabulary of this Celtic proto-language. In the etymologies in this book, Celtic words and word-roots are marked with an asterisk (*), as are hypothetical words and roots in the extinct British (Brythonic) language, which was spoken in Britain two thousand years ago, around the time the Romans conquered the southern part of the island.

The modern Celtic languages form two families: Brythonic, which includes Welsh, Cornish and Breton; and Goidelic, which includes Scottish Gaelic, Manx and Irish. The ancestor languages of these two seem to have arrived in the islands at different times, and probably from different parts of Europe—British from the south in Gaul, and Old Irish from Spain in the West. Welsh, Cornish and Manx derive from the British language, and diverged in the 6th century after Anglo-Saxon armies separated the Cornish and Welsh geographically, and drove another group of Celts across the Channel to Brittany in France. All three of the Goidelic languages derive from the Old Irish language, and were nearly identical until the 13th century.

In the study of Celtic names, it is sometimes difficult to know for certain whether a name comes from a Celtic or a Latin source, since the two languages are related and share some vocabulary. Scholars don't agree, for example, about the origin of the British name, Arthur. It may derive from the Celtic root *artos 'bear'. The Old Irish name Art is from *artos, but Arthur could just as easily be a borrowing of the Latin name Artorius, which is also based on an Indo-European bear word.

Onomastics, the science of the meaning of names, has long been a preoccupation of the Celts. Many early Irish and Welsh tales include explanations of the significance of the names of heroes and heroines like Cú Chulainn, Nessa and Pryderi. There were two early Irish literary genres devoted entirely to explaining the meaning of names: for place names, the *Dindsenchas,* and for the names of people, the *Cóir Anmann.* Cormac mac Cuilennáin, an Irish king and bishop who died in 908, was the author of *Cormac's Glossary,* a work in Old Irish that was Europe's first etymological dictionary.

The study of Celtic languages has received more government and financial support in some regions than in others. This explains in part why we know more about Irish, Scottish and Welsh names than about Cornish, Breton and Manx ones. The scarcity of early Cornish, Breton and Manx documents and literature also has meant that fewer names, and fewer famous bearers of Celtic names, are known from those areas. There is still much work to be done in the study of Celtic names, and many of the etymologies in this book have not been proven correct to everyone's satisfaction, but are simply the most likely possibilities, given the current state of knowledge.

Celtic deity names

Most early Celtic names that are known are those of goddesses and gods. According to ancient Greek and Roman descriptions of the early Continental Celts, their druids knew the Greek alphabet, but refused to use it for any purposes other than keeping accounts. After the Celts began to interact with the Greeks and Romans, however, they made statues of their gods and goddesses, and inscribed their names on them. There were an enormous number of Celtic deities, most of whom were worshipped only in one place. Of the 400 known Celtic deity names, 300 are found only once. The early Celts were a tribal people. The tribal leader, and later the king of the people, was always symbolically married to a goddess of sovereignty, or else the land would cease to be fertile. The importance of tribal gods was long-lasting among the Celts. Even in medieval stories that looked back on the adventures of pagan heroes, characters would commonly say 'I swear by the gods of my tribe' as evidence of their sincerity.

Natural features such as mountains, forests, caves, rivers, springs and other bodies of water had their own deities. Trees and forests were especially sacred to the Celts. There are accounts of early Christian missionaries attacking the pagan Celtic faith by cutting down holy groves of trees. In France, Arduinna was the goddess of the forest of Ardennes, and Vosegus was the god of the Vosges. Two forest deities worshipped in Britain were Nemetona, a goddess whose name means 'sacred grove' and Rigonemetis 'king of the sacred grove'. Gods were associated with specific kinds of trees, for example, Fagus was the god of the beech tree, Vernostonus was the god of the alder, and Callirius was the hazel king.

Nearly every body of water was the abode of a Celtic goddess. Europe's rivers preserve the names of Matrona, goddess of the Marne, Sequanna, goddess of the Seine, and Sinann, goddess of the Shannon, among others. The goddess Danu, or Dôn, an important figure in Irish and Welsh mythology, must have been worshipped throughout Celtic realms, since her name lives on in the names of so many of the rivers of Europe, including the Danube, the Donau and the Don. The Celts also believed that wells and springs were the dwelling places of sacred and powerful beings like Coventina, goddess of holy wells in Scotland, France and Spain, and Sulis, the Celtic goddess of Bath in England. The god Bormo and the goddess Bormana, once worshipped in most of France and part of Spain, have names that mean 'bubbling water'.

Another set of gods have names that refer to light and the color white: Belenus (Fiery One), Loucetis (Bright One) and Vindonnus (Holy Whiteness). The roots of these names turn up later in the names of Irish and Welsh heroes like Beli, Lugh/Lleu, and Finn/Gwyn. The Celts imagined the otherworld as a place of shining, blinding brightness.

Many deities were associated with animals: Artio was a bear goddess, Baco a boar god, Damona a cow goddess, Moccus a pig god. The name of the god Atepomarus means 'very great horse', and the goddess Epona 'divine horse', was adopted by the Roman cavalry. Cunomaglos, the 'lord of the hounds', a god of hunting and healing, was worshipped in Britain. The two elements of his name, reversed, survive today in the Welsh man's name Maelgwn. The word for 'dog' *cú* (genitive *con*) in Old Irish and *ci* (genitive *cun*) in British, occurs frequently in both ancient and modern names like Conor, Conall and Tanguy. This is a dog in the regal sense of a hound, with noble associations.

Some Celtic deities specialized in healing, hunting, poetry or war, while others, such as Lugh and Brigid, had many powers. Judging by the number of places in Europe bearing his name, Lugh was the god worshipped most widely by the Celts. He appears in medieval tales as the Irish Lugh Lámhfhada (Long-Armed Lugh) and the Welsh Lleu Llaw Gyffes (Lleu of the Sure Hand). Lugh's other Irish epithet, Samildanach (Many-Talented) suggests that he may have been the god of all human skills. The early Irish goddess Brigid held dominion over smith-work, poetry and healing. Both Lugh and Brigid (and its Celtic root *brig-*) have remained popular names and name-elements in the modern Celtic languages.

Ancient Celtic names

There are several ways that we know the names of real, historical Celts who lived in Europe two thousand years ago. Some queens, kings and military leaders were mentioned by Greek and Roman writers. The Celts never developed their own alphabet. They used the Latin and Greek alphabets, and two minor alphabets, Lepontic and Galatian, to do their writing, which has come down to us almost entirely as names. Votive tablets are important sources of names. These tablets were thin sheets of metal with inscriptions on them, and they were cast into holy places such as wells, springs and rivers. They carried requests to the gods and goddesses for healing, for benefits, or for revenge. From the writing on these tablets, we know the names of many early Celts who were asking for divine intervention. People also inscribed their names on drinking vessels: 'cup of so-and-so'. We have the names of a large number of Celtic potters because pottery was fired in central kilns, and the makers had to write their names on each piece in order to claim them when they were done.

Early Celtic personal names were composed of word-elements that referred to the natural world, human physical and character traits. Names announced their bearers' fame, strength, valor, brilliance, and beauty. Most of the surviving names are those of men. We know of kings and generals with names like Dumnorix (World King), Luguri (King of Light) and Orgetorix (King of Killers), confirming ancient Greek writers' observation that the Celts were incorrigible boasters. The early Celts bore less presumptuous names as well, such as Suadugeni (Sweet Birth), Sumeli (Good Honey) and Taximaglus (Gentle Prince). Early women's names included Boudicca, derived from a Celtic word meaning 'victory', the name of a queen of the British Iceni who led a rebellion against the Romans in the first century. A queen of the Brigantes, an ally of Rome, was Cartimandua; her name contains the Celtic word for 'little pony'. Elements found in the earliest Celtic names survive to the present day, notably nature words and terms for fire, for light and brightness, for sovereignty and generosity, and for strength, eminence and intelligence.

The fate of Celtic names

Traditional names survived and thrived in Celtic realms until the 16th and 17th centuries. Personal names were associated with ancestors and clan, which were powerful forces in Celtic society. Certain first names were traditional in certain families. What's more, the attitude of the Catholic Church toward naming favored Celtic names, as parents were encouraged to name children after saints. In the early days of Celtic Christianity, thousands of clerics, monks, nuns, abbots, abbesses and bishops became saints, and nearly all these local saints had traditional Celtic names. Some early Celtic saints weren't real people at all, but local deities whose worship was incorporated into Christian ritual. In Brittany, even King Arthur and his sister Morgan la Faye achieved sainthood. Like Celtic deities, early saints, real or not, were associated with wells and other old holy sites, and with pagan rituals such as pilgrimages. Towns and churches were named after saints, keeping their memory alive to the present day. Many saints have traditional feast days, marking the anniversary of their ascent to heaven (March 17 is the feast day of Saint Patrick). Parents often would give a child the name of the saint upon whose feast day it was born.

During the Middle Ages, common European Christian names entered the name stock of Ireland, Scotland, Wales, Cornwall and Man chiefly through the Anglo-Normans, who married into native Celtic families. These imported French names quickly took on a Celtic life of their own, developing new spellings and pronunciations. The Norman French form of William became Liam in Irish, Uilliam in Scottish Gaelic and Gwilym in Welsh, and produced the nicknames Wella in Cornish and Wilmot in Manx. Norman French forms of John and James became the very Irish Seán and Séamus.

The native Celtic names suffered a terrible setback in the 16th and 17th centuries. The Protestant Reformation had an effect on naming everywhere in Western Europe as saints' names, associated with Roman Catholicism, fell out of favor. Names from the Bible became popular instead, and between 1600 and 1750, the native Celtic names almost disappeared in the Protestant regions of Wales, Cornwall, Scotland and the Isle of Man. At the same time, the central governments of Britain and France were attempting to force their Celtic-speaking subjects to adopt the official language, and English or French names as well. Names were assigned to children and adults that sounded something like their native language names, such as Hugh for Aodh in Ireland, Charles for Teàrlach in Scotland, and René for Ronan in Brittany.

Just when Celtic names seemed doomed to oblivion, however, strong cultural and political movements emerged to help revive them.

Beginning in the late 1700s with the publication of James Macpherson's Ossianic poems, there was a resurgence of interest in Celtic culture. Macpherson claimed his poems were genuine 3rd-century literature, but his work was later proven to be a hoax. Macpherson had written the poems himself, based on Scottish folktales and ballads. No matter. The reading public throughout Europe had already become fascinated by Celtic literature and folklore. Scholars and writers collaborated to archive and publish contemporary folktales, legends and ballads, and to translate genuine older literary works. Many Celtic names appeared in print for the first time in centuries, inspiring, as literature so often does, baby naming.

Interest in Celtic culture and language has been closely associated with movements for regional autonomy, beginning in Ireland, the only Celtic region to regain its independence. The Gaelic League, which was formed in 1893 as an organization promoting Irish language and culture, played a major role in this struggle. A founder of the Gaelic League, Douglas Hyde, later became president of independent Ireland.

Nowadays, people choose Celtic names for themselves and their children for different reasons. The choice may be a political statement, a public expression of the desire for independence. Giving a baby a Celtic name can also be a way of honoring one's ancestors. The old Celtic names are unique. They fill a need for expressing individuality as well as the heritage and aspirations of a whole people. They embody the power and endurance of a culture and of a world view that values the natural world along with the human spirit.

SCOTLAND

The residents of the northern part of the island of Britain have had a reputation as fierce warriors ever since the beginning of recorded history. The earliest personal name we know from the region is that of Calgacus, a chieftain who led a confederation of tribes against the Roman army in 83 AD. After a hard-fought victory over Calgacus' troops, the Romans decided it would be a good idea to build walls across the island to protect themselves against the people they called the Picts. Picts was not a name the northern tribes called themselves, but a Latin word meaning 'painted', signifying that they either painted or tattooed their bodies. Too little evidence of the Pictish language remains to determine if it was Celtic or not. Pictish, along with Cumbric, a language closely related to Welsh, were spoken in the south of Scotland until the 9th century. Scottish Gaelic is not closely related to either Pictish or Cumbric. It was brought to Scotland from Ireland in around 500 AD by King Fergus Mòr mac Eirc and his followers. Fergus' kingdom of Dál Ríata already included both northern Ireland and western Scotland, and he was simply moving his capital from one side of the Irish Sea to the other. Ireland and Scotland shared traditions of bardic poetry and literature until the 15th century, although the spoken dialects of the language diverged earlier.

There is no ancient Scottish Gaelic language distinct from the Old Irish language, and many traditional personal names of Scotland derive from Old Irish names. Other names, uniquely Scottish, have their sources in Gaelic words, such as Campbell, from *cam* 'crooked' and *beul* 'mouth'. A great many Scottish names originate in the Gaelic names of places, such as Ailsa, from Ailsa Craig, a rocky island in the Clyde estuary, Logan, from a word meaning 'a hollow', and Kyle, from the Gaelic *caol,* meaning 'a narrow strait'.

Gaelic has never been the only language spoken in Scotland. It became the region's dominant language in around 1100, and went into a decline soon afterwards, so that by 1600 it was spoken only in the Highlands and western islands. Vikings settled the islands and coasts of Scotland during the Middle Ages, and Norse names like Brenda and Ronald were added to the Scottish Gaelic name stock at that time. After the Norman Conquest, French-speaking followers of William the Conqueror were given land in Scotland, and French became an aristocratic language for a time. The surnames of many Norman land-holders evolved into Scottish first names like Fraser and Montgomery. Over the years, many English and Norman French personal names have acquired Gaelic pronunciations and spellings.

Scottish first names became clan names, usually by prefixing the Gaelic word for son, *mac,* to a personal name. Many clans claim descent from an important 'name ancestor'. Clan MacDougal traces its ancestry to Dugall, eldest son of Somerled, Lord of the Isles, who lived in the 12th century. *Nic* is the Gaelic feminine equivalent of *mac,* and means 'daughter of'. It is being used today by a growing number of women in Scotland.

Gaelic names went into a decline in the 16th century when the English authorities began a concerted effort to eradicate Gaelic culture and language. At the same time, a small number of Christian names were replacing native names all across Europe, and in Britain this occurred among the Anglo-Saxons as well as the Celts. This trend also contributed to the disappearance of Gaelic names.

Under a policy of anglicization, Gaelic-speakers were forced to take English names. Often, a completely unrelated English name was assigned, one that sounded somewhat like the given name, such as Rachel for Raonait, or had a similar meaning, like Agnes for Una (both mean 'lamb'). The Gaelic name of the Scottish heroine known in the history books as Flora Macdonald was Fionnuala, a name derived from an Old Irish name meaning 'bright shoulders'. Another sort of anglicization occurred, in which Gaelic names were not changed to other unrelated names, but developed a spelling that was phonetic in English, such as Malcolm for Máel Colm.

The suppression of Gaelic language and culture was followed in the 18th century by a revival of interest throughout Europe. Writers romanticized the Highlands and their picturesque inhabitants, and certain aspects of Gaelic culture were once again a source of pride. The use of Gaelic first names became a way for people to publicly proclaim their Celtic ancestry, both by giving children Gaelic names and by changing their own names to their Gaelic counterparts. For example, the 19th-century poet John Smith took as his pen name Iain Mac a'Ghobhainn (John, Son of the Smith'—*gobha* is Gaelic for blacksmith, and *ghobhainn* is its genitive case).

Naming babies after their grandparents has long been a Gaelic tradition. The mother and father take turns giving children the names of their own parents, then those of aunts and uncles. Another naming tradition—one that is not Gaelic, but has nonetheless added greatly to the number of Gaelic first names—is to give a son or a daughter the mother's maiden name as a first name. In this way, surnames based on Gaelic place names such as such as Blair and Keith have become first names, as have clan names like Fraser and Macaulay. Scottish parents have had a penchant for inventing unique feminine forms of men's names, like Angusina (for Angus) and Donella (for Donald). Literature has had an effect on naming in Scotland as elsewhere, and names that are fairly recent literary inventions, such as Lorna and Fiona, have come to be thought of as venerable Celtic names.

The list that follows contains Gaelic names; non-Gaelic names that developed distinctly Gaelic forms; names closely associated with the culture and history of independent Scotland; and Gaelic surnames and clan names that are commonly used as first names.

Pronunciations are given only for the Gaelic forms of names, since the others have standard English pronunciations. A Gaelic *r* is pronounced like a Spanish *r*, with the tip of the tongue against the palate, behind the front teeth. Syllable emphasis in Gaelic is less than in English, and is more a matter of elongation than of stress.

Adair m. From a surname, which may derive from an early Scottish pronunciation of the English name, Edgar.

Agnes f. After Saint Agnes, from a Greek word meaning 'pure'. Agnes was until recently a favorite name in Scotland. Nicknames for Agnes include **Aggie, Nesta, Nessa, Nessie** and **Segna,** which is Agnes spelled backwards (more or less) following a Scottish folk custom called backspelling.

Aidan m. From Old Irish *áe*d 'fire' + the diminutive *-án*. Aidan is a very old Scottish name. King Aidan mac Gabran, who ruled Argyll in the 6th century, was the first Christian monarch in the British Isles outside Ireland. The 7th-century Saint Aidan established the celebrated monastery of Lindisfarne. His feast day is August 31.

Ailean m. (AY·luhn) From Old Irish *ail* 'noble' + the diminutive *-án*. Anglicized as Alan, a related name from the Breton language. A popular woman's name based on Ailean is **Alana.**

Ailis f. (AY·lees) The Gaelic form of Alice. Nicknames are **Ailie, Alissa** and **Lissa.**

Ailsa f. (AYL·suh) From Ailsa Craig, the name of a rocky island in the Clyde estuary. The name may derive from the Norse *alf* 'elf' + *sigi* 'victory'.

Alasdair m. (AHL·uhs·duhr) The Gaelic evolution of the Greek name Alexander. It became a Scottish royal name in the 12th century when Alexander I ascended the throne. The MacAlisters claim descent from Alasdair Mòr (d. 1299), son of Donald of Islay, Lord of the Isles. Variant spellings include **Alistair, Alastair.** Feminine forms of the name are based on Alexander rather than Alasdair (see Alexandra). The Irish created a pleasing feminine variation, **Alastrina.**

Alexandra f. The feminine form of Alexander. Scottish nicknames include **Alexina, Alexine, Lexie** and **Alexis.**

Alpin m. This name has been used in Scotland from the earliest recorded times until the present, and probably derives from the Latin *albinus* 'white, fair'. It was borne by at least two Pictish kings, and is the source of the surname MacAlpin.

Andreana, Andrina f. Feminine forms of Andrew.

Andrew m. Gaelic **Aindrea** or **Anndra** (AH·oon·druh). From the Greek name, Andreas. Saint Andrew the Apostle is the patron saint of Scotland. A popular nickname is **Drew.**

Angus m. From the Old Irish Óengus: *oen* 'one' + *gus* 'vigor', the name of a god of youth in Irish myth. Angus is a distinctively Scottish first name. The earliest recorded use of the name in Scotland was by an 8th-century Pictish king. It is a traditional first name among the men of clan Donald, whose ancestors include Angus Og of Islay.

Aodh m. (OOH) From the Old Irish *aed* 'fire'. Aodh was one of the most frequent man's names in early Scotland. The surname Mackay is based upon it. The name became anglicized as **Hugh,** and Aodh fell out of favor.

Artair m. (AHR·shtuhr) The Gaelic form of Arthur, from the Celtic **artos* 'bear', or possibly borrowed from the Latin name, Artorius.

Aulay m. From the Norse name Olof. The source of the surname (and first name) Macaulay.

Baird m. From a clan name, derived from the Old Irish *bárd* 'a bard'.

Beathag f. (BAY·hak) From the Gaelic *beatha* 'life'. Bethoc was the name of an 11th-century queen, daughter of Malcolm II. Anglicized as **Betha.**

Blair m. From a surname from Gaelic *blàr* 'plain, field, battlefield'.

Blane m. From the Gaelic *blá* 'yellow'. The name of an important Scottish saint who was Bishop of Kingarth in the late 6th century. Several Scottish churches are named Kilblane in his honor. His feast day is August 11.

Boyd m. Originally a man's nickname derived from the Gaelic *buidhe* 'yellow' or 'fair-haired'.

Brenda f. This name originated in the Shetland Islands, and derives from the Norse *brand* 'sword'. Brenda was the name of the heroine of Sir Walter Scott's novel *The Pirate*.

Bruce m. The name is derived from a surname based on the place name, Braose (now Brieuse) in Normandy, and was brought to

Scotland by the Normans. The most famous Bruce was Robert Bruce, King of the Scots from 1306–29, who liberated Scotland from English rule at the Battle of Bannockburn.

Bryce, Brice m. From the name of the 4th-century Saint Bricius of Tours, France, whose name is Celtic in origin. Bricius' cult was brought to Scotland by the Normans.

Bryson m. From a surname meaning 'son of Bryce'.

Buchanan m. From a surname that was derived from a place name in Stirlingshire. The source of the place name is probably the Gaelic *bocan* 'a young male deer'.

Cailean m. (KAH·luhn) From the Old Irish *cuilén* 'pup, cub, kitten'. This name has been a favorite of the Campbells and MacKenzies. The first Campbell chief of Lochawe, Cailean Mòr, was killed in a battle with the MacDougals in 1294. Since his time, the chief of Clan Campbell has been called MacCailein Mòr 'Son of Big Cailean'. Cailean is often anglicized as **Colin.**

Cairistiona f. (ka·rish·CHE·nuh) The Gaelic form of Christina.

Cairns m. A Gaelic place word that became a surname and eventually a first name. A cairn is a heap of stones traditionally placed on top of a grave.

Calum, Callum m. (KA·luhm) From the Latin *columba* 'dove'. The 6th-century Irish missionary Saint Columba (Colm Cille in Irish) founded a monastery on the Scottish island of Iona that became a great center of learning. Saint Columba's feast day is June 9. Calum is a name in its own right, and is also used as a nickname for Malcolm.

Cameron m. From the Gaelic *cam* 'crooked' + either *shron* 'nose', or possibly *brun* 'hill'. An important clan name, from a place name in the old kingdom of Fife.

Campbell m. From the Gaelic *cam* 'crooked' + *beul* 'mouth'. A clan name that is also used as a first name.

Cathal m. From the Old Irish *cath* 'battle'. This ancient first name is the source of the surname Macall.

Catrìona f. (ka·TREE·uh·nuh) The Gaelic form of Catherine.

Chattan m. A clan name that is used as a first name as well.

Cinàed m. Believed to be Pictish in origin, this name became popular among Gaels in early Scotland. In 843, King Cinàed Mac Ailpín united the Gaels and the Picts in one kingdom, called Scotia. A Gaelic nickname is **Ceanag** (KEN·uhk). Anglicized as **Kenneth** or **Kenny.** A feminine form is **Kenna.**

Ciorstag f. (KER·stuhk) Gaelic nickname for Christine. Anglicized as **Kirstie.**

Coinneach m. (KUH·nyuhx) From the Old Irish name Cainnech, derived from *cáin* 'good, beautiful'. Saint Cainnech founded monasteries in Ireland and Scotland in the 6th century. The city of Kilkenny (Cill Coinneach) in Ireland takes its name from him. His feast day is October 11. The name has been anglicized as **Kenneth, Kenny.**

Conran m. Saint Conran was a 7th-century bishop and apostle to the Orkney Islands. His feast day is February 14.

Craig m. From the Gaelic place word *creag* 'crag, cliff'. Craig is used as a surname and first name in Scotland.

Criostal m. (KREE·uh·stuhl) The Gaelic form of Christopher. This personal name produced the Scottish surnames Chrystal, Cristal and MacCristal.

Dabhaidh m. (DAEE·vee) The Gaelic form of David. Saint David, the son of King Malcolm III and Queen Margaret, was King of the Scots from 1124–53. His feast day is May 24.

Davina f. A Scottish feminine form of David.

Dervorgilla f. From the Old Irish name Der Bforgaill: *der* 'daughter' + Forgall, a god-name. This was one of the most popular Scottish women's names in the Middle Ages. The best-known bearer of the name was the mother of John Balliol, King of Scots. She founded Balliol College, Oxford, in 1250. A modern Irish form of the name is **Dervla.**

Diarmad m. (DYEER·muht) From the Old Irish name, Diarmait, the derivation of which is uncertain. In early Irish literature and in Scottish and Irish ballads and folktales, Diarmaid was a member of the warrior band of Finn mac Cumaill. Diarmaid had a love spot on his face that made women fall instantly in love with him. Clan Campbell traces its ancestry to one Diarmid O'Duibne. Anglicized as **Dermot.**

Dolina, Dona, Donaldina f. These are uniquely Scottish feminine forms of Donald. Nicknames for Dolina are **Dolly** and **Dollag** (DAW·luhk).

Donald m. Gaelic **Dòmhnall** (DAW·nuhl), derived from the Old Irish *domnán* 'world' + *gal* 'valor'. Donald was an early Scottish royal name. Clan Donald, the most powerful of the Highland clans, took its name from a 15th-century Donald, grandson of Somerled, Lord of the Isles.

Donnan m. From the Old Irish *donn,* which means both 'brown' and 'chief' + the diminutive *-án.* The name of a 7th-century abbot of Iona who founded many churches in Scotland. His feast day is April 17.

Dougal m. Gaelic **Dùghall** (DOO·uhl). From the Old Irish name Dubgall: *dubh* 'dark' + *gall* 'a stranger'. A name first used to describe the Danes. Clan MacDougal traces ancestry to Dugall, eldest son of Somerled, Lord of the Isles. Also written **Dugald.**

Douglas m. Gaelic **Dùbhghlas** (DOO·luhs). From the Old Irish *dubh* 'dark' + *glas* 'green or blue'. A common Celtic river name which survives in the names of the rivers Douglas in Ireland and Scotland, Dulas in Wales, and Dawlish, Dowles and Divelish in England.

Drummond m. From a surname based on a clan name that is derived from the name of the village of Drymen in Sterlingshire. The name has been used in Scotland since the 13th century.

Duncan m. Gaelic **Donnchadh** (DOO·nuh·xuh). From the Old Irish *donn* meaning either 'brown' or 'chief' + *cath* 'warrior'. From a surname based on a clan name. Duncan was the name of two early Kings of the Scots. Duncan I, who lived in the 11th century, was immortalized in Shakespeare's *Macbeth.* Clan Donnchadh (the Robertsons) claims Donnchadh Reamhar (Duncan the Stout) as its name ancestor.

Ealasaid f. (ee-AH·luh·sich) The Gaelic form of Elizabeth. Some nicknames with a particularly Scottish flavor are **Elsie, Elspeth,** and **Elspie.**

Edana f. According to some accounts, the 6th-century Irish-born Saint Edana, or **Medana,** founded the convent at Maiden Castle. Legend tells that she took the veil from Saint Patrick himself. The city of Edinburgh formerly bore her name: Dunedin (*dún Edana,* 'Edana's castle'). Her feast day is November 19.

Effie f. Gaelic **Oighrig** (II·rix). A popular Scottish nickname for Euphemia, a name of Greek origin. This name was favored by the nobility from the late Middle Ages until the 19th century.

Eónan m. (YOH·nuhn) From the Old Irish name Adamnan, meaning 'little Adam'. Saint Adamnan (d. 704) was abbot of the important monastery of Iona in Scotland. His writings contain the first mention of the Loch Ness monster.

Erskine m. From a clan name based on the name of a place on the banks of the Clyde, near Glasgow. The derivation of the place name is unknown.

Ewan m. Gaelic **Eòghann** (YOH·uhn). From the Old Irish name Eogán 'born of the yew tree': *éo* 'yew' + *gein* 'birth'. Also written **Ewen, Euen, Euan, Owen,** and anglicized as **Hugh.** This was a traditional name in many clans, including Clan Campbell and Clan Chattan. Ewen of Lochiel, chief of Clan Cameron, was a celebrated opponent of Oliver Cromwell.

Farquhar m. Gaelic **Fearchar** (FER·uh·xuhr), from the Old Irish *fer* 'man' + *cara* 'friendly'. King Ferchar the Long, of Lorne (d. 697), was ancestor of the Chattan and Farquarson clans.

Fenella f. The Gaelic form of the Irish name Fionnuala, from the Old Irish *finn* 'bright, fair' + *gúala* 'shoulders'. Fenella was the name of the heroine of the novel *Peveril of the Peak* by Sir Walter Scott.

Fergus m. Gaelic **Fearghas** (FER·uh·vuhsh). From the Old Irish *fer* 'man' + *gus* 'strength, vigor'. Fergus mac Eirc is considered the ancestor of the Gaels.

Fife, Fyfe m. From a surname derived from the name of an ancient kingdom in eastern Scotland. Some claim the name Fife derives from Fib, the name of one of the seven sons of Cruithne, the legendary ancestor of the Pictish race.

Fingal m. From the Old Irish *finn* 'bright, fair' + *gall* 'stranger'. In his Ossianic poems, 18th-century writer James MacPherson transformed the Irish and Scottish folk hero Finn mac Cumaill into a Scottish king named Fingal.

Finlay m. Gaelic **Fionnlagh** (FYOHN·lax), from the Old Irish *finn* 'bright, fair' + *laoch* 'warrior'. Also written **Finley, Findlay.**

Fiona f. A name invented in the 19th century by the Scottish writer William Sharp, who used it in his pen name, Fiona Macleod. This was a name begging to be invented, since it is a logical feminine form of the Celtic hero-name, Finn. The name Fiona became popular in Scotland, Ireland and beyond.

Flòraidh f. (FLOH·ree) The Gaelic form of the English name, Flora. Flora MacDonald helped Bonnie Prince Charlie escape to the Isle of Skye after his defeat at Culloden, after which Flòraidh became a popular woman's name in the Highlands. Flora was actually an anglicization of MacDonald's Gaelic given name, **Fionnuala.**

Forbes m. Gaelic **Forbeis** (FOR·bish). A clan name from the Gaelic place word *forba* 'field' + the suffix of location *-ais.*

Fordyce m. From a surname based on a place in Banffshire.

Fraser m. From the French surname de Frisselle, which was brought to Scotland by the Normans in the 13th century. Because Fraser sounds like *fraise,* the French word for strawberry, there are strawberry plants on the Fraser coat of arms.

Gabhran m. (GAHV·ruhn) Gaelic for 'little goat'. An ancient Scottish name, borne by a grandson of Fergus mac Erc, the legendary ancestor of the Gaels.

Gavin m. This is the Scottish form of a name that was widely popular in the Middle Ages—as Gawain in England and Gauvain in France. In Arthurian legends and literature, Gawain was one of the boldest knights of the Round Table. Gavin Dunbar was Archbishop of Glasgow and Chancellor of Scotland in the 16th century, and established the first National Court of Justice.

Gilchrist m. From the Gaelic **Gille Criosd** (gil·yuh·KREE·uhst) which means 'servant of Christ'. The name was especially popular during the Middle Ages.

Gillanders m. Gaelic **Gille Anndrais** (gil·yuh·OWN·drish) 'servant of Saint Andrew'.

Gillean m. (GIL·yan) Gaelic **Gilla Eòin** (gil·yuh·YOWN) 'servant of (Saint) John'. The Clan Maclean (son of Gillean) takes it name from the 13th-century warrior, Gillean of the Battle Axe. Gillean is not to be confused with the English woman's name, Gillian (Jillian), which is from Juliana.

Gillespie m. Gaelic **Gilleasbuig** (gil·yuh·IS·pik) 'servant of a bishop'. This is a traditional first name among the Campbells.

Gillis m. Gaelic **Gille Iosa** (gil·yuh·EE·uh·suh) 'servant of Jesus'. This first name is traditional in the Hebrides.

Giorsal f. (GI·ruh·shuhl) The Gaelic form of the name Grace.

Glen m. and f. From the Gaelic place word *gleann* 'valley'.

Gordon m. Gaelic **Gòrdan** (GORSH·tuhn). From a clan name based on a place name in Berwickshire, perhaps derived from the British *gor* 'great' + *din* 'hill-fort'.

Gormla f. (gohr·UHM·luh) From the Old Irish name Gormflaith: *gorm* 'splendid' + *flaith* 'sovereignty'.

Gowan m. From the Gaelic *gobha* 'a smith'. Blacksmiths were very important people in early Celtic culture, often having an aura of magic about them.

Greer m. and f. From a Scottish surname, a contraction of the name Gregor.

Gregor m. Gaelic **Griogair** (GRI·kuhr). The Gaelic form of the name of Saint Gregory of Tours, France. The name was brought to Scotland by the Norman French, and has been widely used as a personal name since the Middle Ages. According to other sources, Gregor is a Gaelic name derived from *greigh* 'a flock or herd'. All forms of this name were officially banned for most of the 17th and 18th centuries because of the alleged misdeeds of some clan members.

Hamish m. (HAY·mish) A Gaelic form of James.

Hugh m. An English name, from the Germanic root *hugi* 'heart, mind'. The name Hugh has traditionally been used in Scotland to anglicize the Gaelic names Eòghann, Uisdeann and Aodh.

Iain m. (EE·ayn) A Gaelic form of John. Also written **Ian.**

Ina f. Originally a nickname for names ending in *-ina,* such as Georgina, Jamesina, and Thomasina, Ina became a popular Scottish girls' name in its own right.

Innes m. and f. The Gaelic word for 'island'. It became a surname and clan name, then a first name.

Iona f. A personal name derived from the name of the island in the Hebrides where Saint Columba founded a monastery in 563.

Iseabail f. (I·shi·bel) The Gaelic form of Isabel, also written **Ishbel.** Many nicknames for Iseabail are used in Scotland, including **Bel, Bell, Bella, Belle, Ella, Ib, Ibbie, Isa, Sib, Tib, Tibbie** and **Tibby.**

Isla f. From the name of the Scottish island, Islay.

Ivar, Ivor m. From the Gaelic form, **Iomhair** (EE·uh·vuhr), of the Old Norse name Ivarr, meaning 'yew tree army'. A traditional first name in clan Campbell of Strachan, and also the source of the surname MacIver.

Jessie f. Gaelic **Seasaidh** (SHAY·see). The Scottish diminutive of the English name Janet. It was popularized by lowland Scots poet Robert Burns.

Jocelin m. and f. A diminutive form of the name of the Breton saint's name, Josse. Norman French settlers brought the name to Scotland, where it has been used since the 12th century.

Keir m. From a clan name, derived from the Old Irish *ciar* 'dark'.

Keith m. From a surname, based on the place name, Ceiteach, in East Lothian.

Kenna f. The feminine form of Kenneth or Kenny (see Coinneach and Cinead).

Kennedy m. From the Old Irish name Cennétig: *cenn* 'head' + *étig* 'ugly'. Although most people associate this name with Ireland, it has been used consistently in Scotland as a family name and first name since the 12th century.

Kentigern m. From the Old Irish *cenn* 'head' + *tigern* 'lord'. The 6th-century Saint Kentigern is the patron saint of Glasgow. He was said to be the son of Owein ap Urien, an early Welsh hero of the Old North. His feast day is January 14.

Kentigerna f. From the Old Irish *cenn* 'head' + *tigern* 'lord'. The name of an Irish queen who traveled to Scotland with her son, Saint Fillan. Kentigerna lived as a recluse on the island of Inchebroida in Loch Lomond, where a church is dedicated to her. Her feast day is January 7.

Kyle m. From a surname based on the Gaelic word *caol* 'narrow', the name of a strait in Ayrshire.

Lachlan m. From Lachlann (LAX·luhn), a Gaelic word formerly used to designate the homeland of the Vikings. The Maclachlans take their name from Lachlan Mòr (Big Lachlan) a chief who lived near Loch Fyne in the 13th century.

Leslie, Lesley m. and f. Possibly from the Celtic **lis* 'court' + **celyn* 'holly'. In Scotland and England, the name is usually spelled Leslie as a man's name and Lesley as a woman's name. In the United States, however, the name is almost always a girls' name, and is usually spelled Leslie.

Lileas f. The Gaelic form of the name Lily, from the Latin *lilium*. Also written **Lilidh** (LI·lee).

Logan m. From a Gaelic place word *lag* 'hollow' + the diminutive suffix -*an*. Logan is used as the name of several places in Scotland, and has been a surname since the 12th century. A very popular name in recent years.

Lorna f. The Scottish writer R.D. Blackmore made up this name for the heroine of his novel *Lorna Doone* (1869). Lorna was a name waiting to be invented, however, since it is makes a lovely and logical feminine form of Lorne.

Lorne m. From a place name in Argyll. Loarn was the name of one of the three sons of the legendary first Gael to arrive in Scotland from Ireland.

Lulach m. (LOO·luh*x*) An old Scottish royal name, meaning 'little calf' in Gaelic, borne by the stepson of Macbeth, who lived in the 11th century.

Macaulay m. From a surname derived from the first name Aulay, 'son of Aulay'.

Macdonald m. 'Son of Donald'. An important clan name, often used in Scotland as a first name.

Màili f. (MAH·lee) A Gaelic nickname for Mary.

Mairead f. (MAY·ret) The Gaelic form of Margaret. The name was wildly popular in the Middle Ages in both Ireland and Scotland, due to widespread admiration for Saint Margaret. Margaret, born to the English royal house of Wessex, married Malcolm III, King of the Scots. She was the mother of three kings as well. Her feast day is June 10.

Màiri f. (MAH·ree) The Gaelic form of Mary. Màiri Mhor nan Oran (Big Mary of the Songs) was a 19th-century Gaelic poet.

Malcolm m. From the Old Irish *máel* 'devotee' + Colm, from the Latin *columba* 'dove'. Colm Cille was the Irish name of the most important early saint in Scotland, known also by the Latin name Columba, who founded the monastery on Iona, and converted the Pictish kings of Scotland. Three medieval kings of the Scots bore the name Malcolm.

Malvina f. A name invented by Scottish writer James Macpherson in his Ossianic poems. Napoleon Bonaparte, a fan of MacPherson, named a group of islands off South America after this literary character. Today the Malvinas are known as the Falkland Islands.

Mariota f. A diminutive of Mary. Mariota was the name of the wife of the great Donald, Lord of the Isles.

Marsaili f. (MAHR·suh·lee) The Gaelic form of Marjorie.

Màrtainn m.(MAHR·shtan) The Gaelic form of Martin.

Mìcheal m. (MEE·hyel) The Gaelic form of Michael.

Mirren m. The modern form of the name of the 6th-century Saint Meadhran, who was active in Strathclyde. Mirren is the patron saint of football. His feast day is September 15.

Montgomery m. The name of a Scottish clan descended from Robert de Montgomerie. The name comes from a French name which in turn is based on a German name, thus it contains the French *mont* 'hill', and the Germanic *guma* 'man' + *ric* 'power'.

Mórag f. (MOHR·ahk) From the Old Irish *mór* 'big'. A classic Gaelic woman's name.

Morven, Morvyn f. Possibly from the Gaelic *mór* 'big' + *bhein* 'peak'. The name of mountains in Aberdeenshire and in Caithness. The word has also been used to designate all of northwest Scotland. Morven recently became a popular name in Scotland.

Muir m. (MYOOR) A surname based on the Gaelic place name *muir* 'a moor'.

Muireall f. (MOOR·uh·yel) From Old Irish *muir* 'sea' + *gel* 'bright, shining'. The name of an heiress of the Thane of Cawdor, who was kidnapped by Sir John Campbell in 1510, and afterwards became the ancestress of the Campbells of Cawdor. The name is anglicized as **Muriel.**

Muirne f. (MOOR·nyuh) An Old Irish word meaning 'beloved', and the name of a character in James Macpherson's Ossianic poems. Anglicized as **Morna.**

Mungo m. The nickname of Kentigern, patron saint of Glasgow, from the Old Irish *mo* 'my' + *cú* 'hound, wolf', and long used as a man's first name.

Munro m. From the clan name Mac An Rothaich, derived from the Gaelic name Rothach, meaning 'a person from Ro'. The Munros are descendants of a family that came from a place near the river Roe in Derry, Ireland.

Murchadh m. (MOOR·uhx) From Old Irish *muir* 'sea' + *cath* 'warrior'. Also written **Murdo, Murdoch.**

Nessa f. A Scottish nickname for Agnes that is used as a name in its own right as well. Nessa is also an Old Irish name.

27

Nevin m. Gaelic **Naomhin** (NUH·veen), from *naomh* 'saint'. This is a traditional first name in Galloway and Ayrshire.

Niall m. (NEEL) An Old Irish name, probably derived from *nél* 'cloud'. Clan MacNeill traces its ancestry to Anrothan, an Irish prince who married a Scottish princess in the 11th century. Anrothan was descended from Irish high king, Niall Naígiallach (Niall of the Nine Hostages), who was claimed as ancestor also by the Irish O'Neill's.

Osla f. A name from the Shetland Islands. It is the Gaelic form of the Norse name Aslaug, meaning 'god-consecrated'.

Ossian m. (UH·sheen) From the Old Irish name Oisín 'little deer'. This character of Irish legend was transformed into a Scottish hero in the Ossianic poems of James Macpherson.

Padruig m. (PA·trik) The Scottish form of the Irish name Pádraig (Patrick). Scottish nicknames include **Padyn, Paton** and **Padan.**

Parlan m. The Gaelic form of the Old Irish name Partholon. This name is the source of the surnames Macfarland and Macfarlane.

Peadair m. (PAY·tuhr) The Gaelic form of Peter.

Pòl m. (PAHL) The Gaelic form of Paul.

Raibeart m. (RAH·bercht) The Gaelic form of Robert. Distinctively Scottish nicknames include **Rab** and **Rabbie.** Clan Robertson takes its name from Robert Riach (Grizzly Robert) who lived in the 15th century.

Ranald, Ronald m. Gaelic **Raghnall** (RUHLL). From the Norse name, Rögnvaldr 'power, might'. A traditional name among the men (and clowns) of the MacDonald clan.

Rhona, Rona f. From the name of a Scottish island, which comes from the Norse *hrauen* 'rough' + *ey* 'island'.

Ronan m. From the Old Irish *rón* 'seal' + the diminutive suffix *-án*. An early Saint Ronan, bishop of Kilmaronen in Lennox, was said to have driven the devil out of the valley of Innerleithen. His feast day is February 7.

Rory m. Gaelic **Ruairidh** (ROO·uh·ree). From the Gaelic *ruadh* 'red'.

Ross m. From the Gaelic place word *ròs* 'upland, promontory'. Ross has been used as a first name in Scotland since the 12th century.

Saraid f. (SAHR·ich) From the Old Irish *sár* 'best, noble'. Sarait, the daughter of the legendary Irish monarch, Conn of the Hundred Battles, was considered the ancestress of the Scottish kings.

Seònaid, Seòna f. (SHAW·nich, SHAW·nuh) The Gaelic version of the English name Joan.

Seumas m. (SHAY·muhs) The Gaelic form of James. Also see Hamish, which is derived from the genitive case of Seumas.

Sholto m. From the Gaelic *sioltaich* 'propagator'. A traditional first name among the Douglases.

Sile f. (SHEE·luh) The Gaelic form of the Latin name Cecilia, and an extremely popular name in Scotland in the early 20th century. Also written **Sheila, Sheelagh** and **Sheelah.**

Simon m. A Hebrew name that has long been used as a first name in Scotland. It is associated especially with Clan Fraser. The chief of Clan Fraser of Loval is called MacShimi 'Son of Simon'. The name is sometimes written **Simeon** or **Symon,** and nicknames include **Sim, Sym** and **Syme.**

Sine f. (SHEE·nuh) The Gaelic form of the English name, Jean. It is also written **Sheena, Sheenagh, Sheenah** and **Shena.**

Somerled m. Gaelic **Somairle** (SOH·uhr·lyuh) From the Old Norse *summarliethi,* 'one who goes forth in the summer', that is, a Viking. According to the Norse *Orkneyinga Saga,* Vikings would spend autumn and winter on the Isle of Man, then raid the near-by coasts of Scotland and Ireland in spring and summer. The name ancestor of Clan Donald was Somerled, Lord of the Isles. This 11th-century chieftain was half-Gaelic, half-Norse, and ruled of the Isle of Man, the southern Hebrides and Argyll. The name is anglicized as **Sorley.**

Sorcha f. (SOHR·uh·xuh) From the Old Irish *sorchae* 'bright, radiant'. This name has been popular in both Scotland and Ireland.

Stewart, Stuart m. Gaelic **Stiùbhart.** Originally an occupational name, borne by the keepers of the Scottish royal household. It was later changed to a hereditary family name, then it became a royal name as the House of Stuart ruled Scotland beginning in 1371, and England from 1603–1714. It is used as a first name for boys, and occasionally for girls.

Struan m. (STROO·uhn) Perhaps from Gaelic *struan* 'stream'. This was once a common name among the men of Clan Donnchaidh (the Robertsons), who owned the lands of Struan in Perthshire.

Teàrlach m. (CHAR·luh*x*) A Gaelic word meaning 'well-shaped'. A name popular among the Stewarts. It was often anglicized as the unrelated name, Charles.

Tòmas, Tàmhas m. (TAW·muhs) The Gaelic form of Thomas.

Torquil, Torkill m. Gaelic **Torcaill** (TOHR·kil), from a Norse name based on the god-name Thor. Torquil was the name of the founder of Clan MacLeod of Lewis, and has been a popular name for the men of that clan.

Uilleam m. (OOL·yuhm) The Gaelic form of William, brought to Scotland in the Middle Ages by the Norman French companions of William the Conqueror. **Liam,** the Irish form of the name, is also popular in Scotland.

Uisdean m. (OOS·juhn) Gaelic form of Austin, from Augustine.

Una f. From the Old Irish *uan* 'lamb.' In Scotland, this name was often anglicized as Agnes, which means 'lamb' in Greek.

Wallace m. The origin of this name is the Anglo-Saxon word *walas* or *wealas* 'a Celt', source also of the words Wales and Welsh. It first came into use as a surname, in the border regions of Scotland, and began to be used as a first name in memory of the Scottish national hero William Wallace, who was executed by British authorities in 1305.

Walter m. Gaelic **Bhàtar** (VAH·tuhr). From the Germanic *wald* 'rule' + *harja* 'folk.' The name is usually associated with the eminent Scottish writer, Sir Walter Scott (1771–1832). Walter has been moderately popular as a first name in Scotland.

IRELAND

he Irish people were the third in Europe, after the Greeks and Romans, to develop a written literature in their own language. It is said that when the Irish converted to Christianity, they were appalled to find that they were not mentioned in the Bible, and they lost no time recording their own history to make up for this oversight. Early Irish writings that have survived to the present include poetry, myth, legend, biography and history, and from these we know that there were well over 10,000 different personal names in use before the Middle Ages. Many of these early names were composed of one or two word-elements with clear meanings, such as the names of animals, plants, colors, and personal qualities, both physical and moral. *Muir* 'sea' and *gel* 'bright, shining' combined to form the name Muiríol, and *síth* 'peace' and *maith* 'good' were used to create a name that became Síomha in Modern Irish. We don't know exactly how or why these names were bestowed long ago. The characters of early Irish legend often changed their names as they passed from childhood to adulthood. Two genres of Irish literature, *Dindsenchas* and *Cóir Anmann,* explained, quite unscientifically, the origins and meanings of the names of places and people.

Irish names have changed over time along with the language, for Modern Irish differs significantly from Old Irish, just as Italian differs from Latin. A name may have two or more historical forms as well as modern anglicized spellings, for example, the Old Irish name Cáemgen became Modern Irish Caoimhín, anglicized as Kevin. In the process of anglicization, Irish personal names have been rendered more like English ones. This has happened in two ways. Some Irish names have developed alternate spellings that are more phonetic in English, such as Maeve for Meadhbh and Cliona for Clíodhna. The other type of anglicization came about as part of the suppression of the Irish language by English authorities, beginning in the 17th century. Irish speakers were required to speak English and use English names for all official purposes, and as a result, people were assigned English first names that sounded something like their Irish names, but which were completely unrelated, such as Hugh for Aodh, or Grace for Grania. Certain Irish personal names were traditional in certain families, as noted for many of the names below, and when these families were required by the Penal Laws to use English names, the new names were passed on in the traditional manner. In this way, anglicized names like Myles and Malachy gradually came to seem Irish because they were associated with so many famous Irish men and women. Anglicized forms are given for many of the names below, both for historical interest and so that parents will have a choice of ways to spell a child's name.

Irish versions of European Christian names like Seán and Sinéad have also come to be thought of as quintessentially Irish. These names were brought to Ireland in the 12th century by invaders and settlers from England who were descendants of the Norman companions of William the Conqueror. Seán is from the Norman French name Jehan, Sinéad from Jonet.

Irish is now the official first language of the country of Ireland, and all young people must study the language in school. Most of the nation's business is conducted in English, however, and few people are fluent in Irish. Still, it has become a matter of pride to return to older names, both for oneself and for one's children. The Modern Irish spellings of these names, complete with accents, are used mainly by the people of the Gaeltacht (the predominantly Irish-speaking areas) and by artists and intellectuals. Some people have adopted the Irish form of their English given name, such as Tomás for Thomas or Pádraigin for Patricia. More and more parents throughout Ireland are choosing the old traditional names for their children, though most of them choose an anglicized spelling, such as Cliona, instead of Modern Irish Clíodhna, Orla rather than Orlaith.

The Irish and Scottish began using hereditary surnames before most other Europeans. They were already identifying themselves by both their personal and clan names, so it was a simple matter to make these clan names into hereditary last names. A majority of Irish surnames were created from personal names by adding *mac* or *mc,* meaning son, or *ó* (originally *ua*) meaning 'grandson or descendant of'. Later, many Irish families dropped these prefixes altogether. There isn't really any difference between prefixes *mac* and *ó,* and there are about an equal number of Irish last names that contain each one. First names underwent transformations in spelling and sound when they became parts of surnames, and changed from nominative case to genitive. For example, the name Conn (pronounced KOHN) became the surname mac Coinn (pronounced MAK KOOIN), which was anglicized as Quinn. The Irish language also contains a surname prefix *ni* 'daughter of', and many Irish women today are choosing to incorporate this into their last names. Irish surnames are patronymic, based on the name of the father or of a male ancestor. Two exceptions are the names of the legendary heroes Conchobar mac Nessa (Nessa was his mother) and Conán mac Morna (son of the woman Morna).

The Irish and English languages are very different from one another in vocabulary, grammar and pronunciation. The sounds of Irish are not easy for an English speaker to hear and repeat, since they are elusively betwixt and between familiar English consonants and vowels. The *r* in Máire, for example, is pronounced something like the *s* in pleasure and something like a Spanish *r.* Syllable stress is less emphatic in Irish than in English, and is more a matter of lengthening than emphasis.

The spelling of Modern Irish presents a great challenge to the uninitiated. In the following list, the Modern Irish spelling of a name is given first if it looks to an English speaker somewhat like it sounds. For other names, an anglicized spelling is given first—Tara first, rather than Teamhair, for example. The names of early saints and of characters from myth and legend are typically written using their Old Irish spellings, which are often different from the Modern Irish. The pronunciations given for the names are only approximations of Irish pronunciation, since there are regional differences. You will probably want to change the pronunciation to what you consider a nice-sounding name in your part of the world, knowing that it isn't exactly what it would be in Ireland. If American parents choose the name Caitlin, for example, they will have to fight to get people to pronounce it in the proper Irish way, kayt·LEEN, rather than KAYT·lin.

Ailbhe m. and f. (AL·fe) From the Old Irish name, Ailbe, from the Celtic *albho* 'white'. Legends tell of two women bearing the name. One was a daughter of the fairy king Midir. The other, Ailbe Grúadbrecc (Freckled Ailbe) was daughter of the King Cormac mac Airt and wife of Finn mac Cumaill. Saint Ailbe, who lived in the 6th century, was raised by a wolf, according to an early account of his life. His feast day is September 12. A nickname for Ailbhes who are men is **Alby**.

Ailbhis m. (AL·vis) A 6th-century Irish saint; perhaps another form of Ailbhe. Anglicized as **Elvis.**

Ailín m. (ay·LEEN) An early Irish name, probably derived from Old Irish *ail* 'noble'.

Ailionóra f. (e·le·NOH·ra) The Irish form of Eleanor.

Ailís f. (AY·lish) The Irish form of Alice, derived from the Norman French name Aliz.

Áine f. (AW·ne) From the Old Irish *áine* 'brilliance, wit, splendor, glory'. In legend, Áine was the daughter of Fer I (Man of the Yew) and queen of the fairies of south Munster. She was believed to dwell at the place now called Knockany (*Cnoc Áine*, 'Áine's Hill').

Aisling f. (AH·shleeng) From the Old Irish *aislinge* 'dream, vision'. This was once a man's name, but is currently popular as a woman's name. It is also written **Ashling.**

Alastar m. (AH·lah·star) The Irish form of the Greek name Alexander, introduced into Ireland via Scotland, where the modern Gaelic form is Alasdair.

Amargein m. (aw·VEER·een) From the Old Irish *amar* 'singing, song' + *gein* 'birth'. The most celebrated bearer of this name was the druid, poet and judge of the Sons of Mil, legendary ancestors of the Irish. It was Amargein who pronounced the first judgment given on Irish soil, and his magic ensured that the Sons of Mil would triumph over the Tuatha Dé Danann. A traditional name in the O'Clery family.

Ana f. (AW·ne) An Old Irish goddess name. Ana, or **Anu,** also known as **Dana**, or **Danu,** was the mother goddess of the mythic early settlers of Ireland, the Tuatha Dé Danaan.

Aodh m. (AY) From the Old Irish *áed* 'fire'. Another name of the god Dagda in Irish myth. This was one of the most common men's names in early Ireland, borne by six high kings and twenty saints. Aodh was the name of two Irish rebels in the time of Queen Elizabeth I, Aodh (Hugh) O'Neill and Aodh Rua (Red Hugh) O'Donnell. Anglicized as **Hugh**.

Aodhán m. (AY·dawn) From the Old Irish name Áedán, diminutive of *áed* 'fire'. Áedán was the name of 21 early Irish saints. It is a popular name, and is often anglicized as **Aidan** (AY·dahn).

Aoife f. (EE·fe) From the Old Irish Aífe, a goddess name meaning 'beautiful, radiant'. In a tale of the apprenticeship of the Ulster hero Cú Chulainn, Aífe was the fiercest woman warrior in the world. After she was defeated by the hero, she bore him his only son, Connla. Aoife is currently a very popular Irish name.

Aonghus m. (AYNG·guhs) From the Old Irish *oen* 'one' + *gus* 'vigor'. In Irish myth, Óengus was a god of youth and love, the son of the goddess Boand and the god Dagda. Óengus Tírech was the name of a legendary hero, said to be the ancestor of the O'Briens and MacNamaras. Five saints bore this name, including Óengus Ceile Dé, whose feast day is March 11. Anglicized as **Angus**.

Ardál m. (AHR·dawl) From the Old Irish *art* 'bear' + *gal* 'fury, valor'. This was a traditional name in the MacMahon, O'Connelly, MacCabe, McKenna and MacArdle families.

Art m. (ART) From the Old Irish *art* 'bear'. This is an ancient Irish name, not a nickname for for the English name Arthur (though both derive from a common Indo-European bear word **arth*). According to legend, Art Óenfer (Art the Lonely) was a high king of Ireland and father of Cormac mac Airt. A later, historical Art was Art McMurrough, a medieval king of Leinster who fought the English. The name Art was traditional among the O'Haras, MacMurroughs, O'Connors, O'Mulloys, O'Rourkes, O'Neills, MacKiernans, and O'Keeffes. A nickname is **Artagán.**

Artúr m. (AR·toor) The Irish form of the British name Arthur, first recorded in Ireland in the 9th century.

Bairre, Barra m. (BAW·re) A nickname for Bearach and Finnbarr, also used as a name in its own right. Anglicized as **Barry**.

Beacán m. (BA·kawn) From Old Irish *bec* 'little' + the diminutive *-án*. Saint Becan founded a monastery in Westmeath in the 6th century. His feast day is May 26.

Bearach, Berach m. (BA·rax) From the Old Irish *berach* 'pointed, sharp'. Berach was the name of many Irish saints, including the patron saint of the O'Hanlys, whose feast day is February 15.

Bearchán m. (BAR·uh·hawn) The diminutive of Bearach. Bearchán was a common name in early Ireland, borne by numerous saints, including Bearchán of Inishmore in Galway, whose feast day is April 6.

Bevin f. (BAY·vin) From the Old Irish *bé* 'woman' + *binn* 'sweet, melodious'. This was the name of several early Irish queens and saints, including a 12th-century abbess of Derry. Modern Irish **Bébhinn.**

Binne f. (BEE·ne) From the Old Irish *binn* 'melodious, sweet'. Binne was the name of several fairy women in legend.

Bláithín f. (BLAW·heen) From the Old Irish *bláth* 'flower'.

Blathmac m. (BLAW·vak) From the Old Irish *bláth* 'flower' + *mac* 'son'. This was a popular name in early Ireland. Blathmacc mac Con Brettan was an 8th-century poet.

Bran m. (BRAWN) From the Old Irish *bran* 'raven'. Bran was the name of a pagan Celtic god, known in both Irish and Welsh myth. The early Irish literary work, *The Voyage of Bran, Son of Febal* recounts Bran's journey from Ireland to the otherworld Island of Joy and Land of Women. A very popular in the Middle Ages, and traditional among the O'Byrnes.

Brandubh m. (BRAWN·doov) From the Old Irish *bran* 'raven' + *dubh* 'black'. Brandubh was the name of a medieval king of Leinster and of two saints, whose feast days are February 6 and June 3.

Breandán m. (BRAWN·dan) Possibly a borrowing of the Welsh word *brenhin* 'king'. According to a medieval Latin tale, *The Voyage of Saint Brendan,* the 6th-century Irish saint known as Brendan the Navigator explored regions perhaps as far away as North America in a leather-clad boat, or curragh. Saint Brendan's feast day is May 16. Breandán is a perennially popular Irish name. Anglicized as **Brendan.**

Brian m. (BREE·an) The derivation of the name is not certain, but may be from the Celtic **brig* 'high, noble'. In Irish myth, Brian was one of the three sons of the goddess Danu of the Tuatha De Dánaan. The most celebrated historical Brian was high king Brian Boru, who ruled Ireland from 1002 to 1014 and defeated the Vikings at the battle of Clontarf. The name was traditional among the O'Connors, MacDonaghs, MacGoverns, O'Kellys and MacMahons.

Briana f. (BREE·a·na) A feminine form of Brian.

Bríd, Bríghid f. (BREED, BRI·jid) An Old Irish goddess name from the Celtic **brig* 'high, mighty'. The most famous woman saint of Ireland is Brigid, who was abbess of Kildare, previously the site of the shrine of a pagan goddess of the same name. According to myth, there were three sister goddesses of the Tuatha Dé Danaan named Brigid: the goddess of poetry, the goddess of healing, and the goddess of smith work. Also written **Bride, Brigid, Brigit, Bridget.** Nicknames include **Bridie, Bidelia, Bidina,** and **Breda.** Saint Brigid's feast day is February 1, or Imbolc in the old calendar. She is the patron saint of scholars.

Bryg f. (BREE) From the same Celtic root as Bríd, **brig* 'high, mighty'. This name was borne by thirteen early saints.

Cairbre m. (KAHR·bre) Cairbre was the first of the legendary Sons of Mil to settle in Ireland. There were two noted saints by this name. One was Bishop of Assaroe (feast day November 1); the other was Bishop of Moville (feast day May 3).

Caíreach f. (KEE·re*x*) From the Old Irish name Caírech. Saint Caírech Dergáin is the patron saint of the women in the Kelly and Madden families. Her feast day is February 9.

Caireann f. (KAW·ran) Cairenn Chasdubh (Cairenn of the Dark Curly Hair) was mother of Niall of the Nine Hostages, legendary ancestor of the O'Neill family and of the high kings of Ireland.

Caitríona f. (kaw·TREE·a·na) The Irish form of Catherine, a name brought to Ireland by the Anglo-Normans. Nicknames include **Caít** (KAYT), **Cáitín** (kay·TEEN), **Caitlín** (kayt·LEEN), and **Tríona** (TREE·a·na).

Caoilinn f. (KAY·leen) From the Old Irish name Cáelfind: *cáel* 'slender' + *finn* 'bright, fair'. Saint Cáelfind of Kerry has her feast day February 3.

Caoilte m. (KWEEL·te) According to legend, Caílte was a member of Finn mac Cumaill's warrior band. In the medieval tale, *Colloquy of the Ancients,* Caílte returned from the otherworld to tell Saint Patrick stories of Finn mac Cumaill and the other heroes of old pagan Ireland.

Caoimhín m. (kwee·VEEN) Old Irish Cáemgen: *caem* 'beautiful' + *gein* 'birth'. In the 7th century, Saint Cáemgen established the famous monastery at Glendalough in County Wicklow. His feast day is June 3. This is a perennially popular name in Ireland, and is anglicized as **Kevin.**

Cass m. (KAHS) From the Old Irish *cas* 'curly'. A popular name in early Ireland. Cass was the name of a legendary ancestor of the O'Briens, MacNamaras and O'Gradys.

Cathal m. (KOH·hal) From the Old Irish *cath* 'battle'. A popular name in the early Middle Ages. Cathal Crobderg (Red-Handed Cathal) was a king of Connacht in the 13th century. A traditional name in the MacManus, Maguire and MacDonagh families.

Ceallachán m. (CAL·a·*x*awn) The meaning of this name is not certain: it may mean 'someone who frequents churches' or 'someone who is warlike'. The name was borne by a 10th-century king, and by a saint whose feast day is April 22. Anglicized as **Callaghan.**

Ceara f. (KE·a·ra) From the Old Irish name, Cera, the meaning of which may be 'bright red'. Cera was the name of a wife of Nemed, one of the legendary early invaders of Ireland.

Cearbhall m. (KEE·a·ruhl) From the Old Irish name, Cerball. The name was borne by early kings of Ossory and Leinster, and was traditional among the O'Dalys. Cearbhall Ó Dalaigh was a president of the Irish Republic. Anglicized as **Carroll.**

Cessair f. (KAH·seer) In legend, Cessair, the granddaughter of Noah, was said to have led the first settlers to Ireland—a band of fifty women and three men whom Noah had allegedly refused to allow onto the ark. With the exception of Finian, all of Cessair's people perished in a great flood.

Cian m. (KEE·an) From the Old Irish *cían* 'ancient, enduring'. In legend, Cian was the son of Dian Cécht, the god of healing of the Tuatha De Dánaan. He was also the father of the hero Lugh. The name was traditional among the O'Haras and O'Garas, who considered another Cian, the son of Ailill Olom, their ancestor. Cian is currently a popular name.

Ciar f. (KEE·ar) From the Old Irish *ciar* 'dark'. Saint Ciar of Killkeary has two feast days, January 5 and October 16.

Ciarán m. (KEER·an) From the Old Irish *ciar* 'dark' + *-án,* the diminutive suffix. The 6th-century Saint Ciarán founded the monastery of Clonmacnoise. His feast day is September 9. A popular name, often anglicized as **Kieran.**

Cliona f. (KLEE·a·na) From the Old Irish name Clídna. In legend, Clídna was the name of one of three beautiful daughters of the poet of Manannán mac Lir. A fairy of the same name was the guardian spirit of the MacCarthys. Currently a popular name. Modern Irish **Clíodhna.**

Clodagh f. (KLOH·da) A popular girls' name in Ireland, from the name of a river in Tipperary.

Cochrann f. (KAW·kran) From the Old Irish *coch* 'red', possibly meaning 'a red-haired woman'. In legends of Finn mac Cumaill, Cochrann was the mother of the irresistible Diarmaid.

Coinneach m. (KI·ne*x*) From the Old Irish name Cainnech, from *cáin* 'good, beautiful'. The 6th-century Saint Cainnech founded monasteries in Scotland and Ireland, including Aghaboe in County Laois. The city of Kilkenny takes its name from him. Saint Cainnech's feast day is October 11. The name is anglicized as **Kenneth** or **Kenny.**

Colm, Colum m. (KUHL·uhm) From the Latin *columba* 'dove'. The 6th-century Saint Colm Cille (Columba) 'dove of the church' is one of the most important Irish saints, along with Patrick and Brigid. Born in Donegal to a branch of the royal Uí Neill clan, Colm Cille was banished to Scotland, allegedly for copying a book without its owner's permission. There, he founded the celebrated monastery of Iona and also converted the pagan kings of Scotland to Christianity. His feast day is June 9. A classic Irish man's name.

Colmán m. (KOHL·mawn) The diminutive of the name Colm, above. According to early records, there were more than 200 Irish saints by this name! Colmán was the given name of Irish-born Saint Columbanus (ca. 543–615), who founded several of the most renowned monasteries of Europe, including Luxeuil in France and Bobbio in Italy. His feast day is November 23.

Conaire m. (KAW·ni·re) An ancient Irish name, perhaps from *cú (con)* 'wolf, hound' + *aire* 'farmer, landowner'. This is a name associated mainly with legendary Irishmen, notably Conaire Mór (Big Conaire), high king and hero of the tale, *The Destruction of Da Derga's Hostel.* He was said to be the son of a princess and a bird-man, and it was forbidden for him to hunt birds.

Conall m. (KAW·nal) From the Old Irish *cú (con)* 'hound, wolf'. Many celebrated Irishmen, real and fictional, bore the name Conall. Conall Cernach was a legendary hero of Ulster. Conall Gulban was the great-grandfather of Saint Colm Cille and the ancestor of the O'Donnells, O'Gallaghers and O'Dohertys.

Conán m. (KOH·nawn) From Celtic **kuno* 'great, high'. In legends and folktales, Conán mac Mórna was a member of Finn mac Cumaill's warrior band. Six Irish saints bore the name as well.

Conley, Conleth m. (KAWN·lay, KOHN·leth) An old and rare name. The most famous bearer of the name was Conláed, a 6th-century bishop of Kildare, head of the school of manuscript illumination there. His feast day is May 3.

Conn m. (KOHN) An ancient Irish name, possibly derived from *cú (con)* 'hound, wolf'. In legend, Conn Céthchathach (Conn of the Hundred Battles) was a high king of Ireland. He is claimed as ancestor by the O'Neills, O'Donnells, O'Connors, O'Rourkes, O'Flahertys and O'Dowds.

Conor, Connor m. (KAW·nor) From the Old Irish Conchobar: *cú (con)* 'hound, wolf' + *cobar* 'desiring'. In the Irish epic, *The Cattle Raid of Cooley*, Conchobar mac Nessa was king of Ulster. The name Conor is quite popular today. The Modern Irish form is **Conchobhar** (KROO·ar).

Conrí m. (KAWN·ree) From the Old Irish *cú (con)* 'hound, wolf' + *rí* 'king'. One of the earliest recorded Irish men's names.

Cormac m. (KAWR·mak) A popular name in Ireland since earliest times. Cormac mac Airt was a legendary high king of Ireland, ancestor of the O'Neills. Cormac was also the name of many real kings, bishops and saints.

Criofan m. (KREE·fan) From the Old Irish name Crimthann, 'a fox'. Crimthann was the name of ten of Finn mac Cumaill's warriors, and of one Saint Crimthann, whose feast day is May 23.

Cú Chulainn m. (KOO *X*UHL·in) The name of the hero of the early Irish epic, *The Cattle Raid of Cooley*. Cú Chulainn is Ireland's greatest legendary hero, along with Finn mac Cumaill. Finn has long been a popular man's name in Ireland, but Cú Chulainn has not. Cú Chulainn's birth name was Setanta, and he was given his adult name after he killed the watchdog of the smith, Culann. He then assumed the dog's place and duties, and was renamed Cú Chulainn 'hound of Culann'. Other early Irish names that begin with cú are Cú Maige (Hound of the Plain), Cú Mara (Hound of the Sea) and Cú Coigríche (Hound of the Border). These were used as personal names in many families, then fell out of use during the Middle Ages.

Dáire m. (DII·re) An Old Irish word meaning 'fruitful', and most likely the name of an early god. Anglicized as **Darragh.**

Dáirine f. (daw·REE·ne) From the Old Irish *dáire* 'fruitful'. The name of a legendary princess of Tara.

Dealla f. (DAW·la) The name of a legendary early invader of Ireland, a companion of the woman leader Cessair.

Declán m. (DEK·lawn) Declán was the name of a 6th-century saint who founded the monastery of Ardmore in County Waterford. His feast day is July 24. Currently a popular name.

Deirdre f. (DYEER·dre) An Old Irish name that has become quite popular in the 20th century in Ireland and beyond. According to the early Irish tale, *The Exile of the Sons of Uisliu,* Deirdre was the daughter of Feidlimid, who was King Concobar's storyteller. The druid Cathbad predicted her birth, her great beauty and the sorrow she would bring to Ulster. An interesting older spelling is **Derdriu.**

Dervil f. (DER·uh·vil) From the Old Irish name Derbáil, probably derived from *der* 'daughter' + *Fál,* an ancient name for Ireland. Several early and medieval Irish princesses were named Derbáil, and the name was traditional among the McDermotts. Modern Irish **Dearbháil** is currently a popular girls' name, and is also written **Dervla** (DAYR·vla).

Desmond m. (DEZ·mond) From a surname based on an old name for the territory of South Munster.

Devnet f. From the Old Irish *damnat* 'little doe'. Damnat, queen of Munster, was the legendary ancestor of the O'Cahills, O'Flynns and O'Moriartys. Modern Irish **Damhnait** (DOW·net).

Diarmaid m. (DEER·mit) From the Old Irish name Diarmait. In legends and folktales, Diarmaid was a member of the warrior band of Finn mac Cumaill. He had a mark on his face that caused women to fall instantly and madly in love with him. Diarmaid was a traditional name in the McCarthy, McDermott, O'Brien and O'Connor families. Currently a popular name. Anglicized as **Dermot.**

Doireann f. (DAHR·an) From the Old Irish name Doirend, possibly meaning 'daughter of Finn'. One legendary Doirend was the daughter of the fairy king Midir, another was the granddaughter of the pagan god Dagda. Anglicized as **Dorren.**

Dónal m. (DOH·nal) From the Old Irish name Domnall: *domun* 'world' + *gal* 'ardor, valor'. One of the most popular Irish names since earliest times. Domnall was the name of five high kings including Domnall Ilchelgach (Dónal of the Many Treacheries), ancestor of the O'Neills and the MacLoughlins.

Donn m. (DOWN) From the Old Irish *donn,* which means both 'brown' and 'chief'. In myth, Donn, the god of the dead, lived on an island off the coast of Munster. Despite its association with the netherworld, this name was popular in Ireland until the end of the 19th century, particularly among the Maguires and the Kennedys. A nickname is **Donnagán.**

Donnchadh m. (DOH·nuh·*x*a) From the Old Irish name Donnchad: *donn* 'brown' or 'chief' + *cath* 'battle'. This was the name of the son of Brian Boru, King Donnchad Donn, who died in 1064. This was a traditional name in the O'Brien family. Anglicized as **Donagh** (DOH·na).

Dubhdara m. (doov·DAW·ra) From the Old Irish *dub* 'dark' + *dara* 'oak'—'dark man of the oak'.

Dubheasa f. (doo·VAH·sa) From the Old Irish *dub* 'dark' + *ess* 'waterfall', probably meaning 'dark lady of the waterfall'.

Éabha f. (AY·va) From the Old Irish name Éva. According to legend, Éva was one of the wives of Nemed, an early invader of Ireland.

Eachna f. (A*X*·na) From the Old Irish *ech* 'horse'. In early legend, a Connacht princess named Eachna was one of the loveliest and cleverest women in the world.

Eadan f. (AH·dan) From the Old Irish name Etan, borne in one tale by the beloved of the hero Cú Chulainn.

Éamon, Éamonn m. (AY·mon) The Irish version of the Anglo-Saxon name Edmund. American-born Éamon de Valera (1882–1975) served as both president and prime minister of the Irish Republic.

Eavan f. (E·van) From the Old Irish *aibinn* 'fair form'. The name of several legendary Irish princesses. Modern Irish **Aoibheann.**

Eíbhlin f. (ay·LEEN) From the French Aveline, a name brought to Ireland by the Anglo-Normans, and very popular among the nobility in the Middle Ages.

Eilís f. (AY·leesh) The Irish form of Elizabeth. Also written **Eilise.**

Éireamhón m. (AY·ra·vohn) From the Old Irish name, Érémon. According to legend, Érémon led the expedition of the Sons of Mil to Ireland to avenge his uncle Ith, who had been slain by the Tuatha Dé Danann. This would make Érémon the chief ancestor of the Irish people. A traditional name in the McSweeney and O'Halloran families.

Eithne f. (AY·he·ne) This early Irish name has become popular again today. A mythical Eithne was the mother of the god Lugh. Eithne was also the name of many legendary queens, including the wives of Conn of the Hundred Battles and Cormac mac Airt. Eight saints also bore the name. Anglicized as **Ethna** (ET·na), **Enya** (EN·ya).

Elatha m. and f. (AHL·a·hah) An old name meaning 'art or craft'.

Émer f. (EE·mer) According to legend, Émer was the wife of the great hero Cú Chulainn. When he came courting, Emer refused to marry him until he answered a series of riddles, for she would only marry the man who was her equal in noble birth, beauty and wisdom. William Butler Yeats' play, *The Only Jealousy of Emer,* retells her story.

Eochaid m. (OH·xad) From the Old Irish *ech* 'horse'. The name may mean 'horse rider'. Many real and legendary kings bore this name, for horses were symbols of kingship in early Irish culture. There was also a Saint Eochaid who was bishop of Tallaght (feast day January 28) and another who was abbot of Lismore (feast day April 17). Modern Irish **Eochaidh.**

Eocho m. (OH·xoh) A nickname for Eochaid that became a name in its own right. Eocho mac Tairdelbaig was an ancestor of the O'Hallinan and O'Quinn families.

Eoghan m. (OHN) From the Old Irish name Eogán 'born of the yew tree': *éo* 'yew' + *gein* 'birth'. Eogán was the name of several early kings and saints. Eogán mac Damthacht was a celebrated Ulster hero. The earliest Saint Eoghan was a 6th-century bishop of Tyrone, and the uncle of Saint Kevin. His feast day is August 23. Eoghan is currently a popular name.

Eoin m. (OH·een) The Irish form of the Latin Johannes. The Irish names Eoin and Seán are both derived from this Latin name. Seán, from the French Jehan, and was introduced into Ireland by the Norman French many centuries after Johannes became an Irish name. Eoin is currently a popular name.

Étaoin f. (AY·deen) From the Old Irish *ét* 'jealousy'. This legendary heroine surpassed all other women in beauty and gentleness. She was the heroine of an early Irish tale, *The Wooing of Etain,* which tells of the competition for her love between the fairy king Midir and the mortal king Eochaid Airem. This name was traditional in the O'Connor, O'Hara and O'Flannagan families. Currently a popular name.

Faolán m. (FAY·lawn) From the Old Irish *faol* 'wolf' + the diminutive *-án*. Faolán was the name of fourteen Irish saints, as well as ten warrior of Finn mac Cumaill's outlaw band. It is the source of the surnames Phelan and Whelan. Anglicized as **Fallon.**

Fearghus m. (fay·REES) From the Old Irish *fer* 'man' + *gus* 'strength, vigor'. Fergus mac Róich, the foster-father of Cú Chulainn, was one of the heroes of the Irish epic, *The Cattle Raid of Cooley.* He was renowned for his strength and stamina both on the battle-field and in the bedroom. Fergus Fínbél (Fergus Wine-Mouth) was poet of the Fiana. A classic Irish name, anglicized as **Fergus** (FER·guhs).

Fergal m. (FAYR·gal) From the Old Irish *fer* 'man' + *gal* 'fury, valor'. Fergal mac Máel Dúin was yet another ancestor of the O'Neills. This name was popular in the MacNamee and O'Boyle families.

Fianait, Fionnait f. (FYAN·it) An Old Irish word for 'deer'. There were two early saints by this name. Their feast days are January 4 and November 29.

Fidelma f. (fee·DEL·ma) From the Old Irish name, Fedelm. Fedelm Noíchrothach (Fedelm Nine-Times-Beautiful), the daughter of King Conchobar mac Nessa of Ulster, was a woman warrior. There were also six Irish saints by this name. Modern Irish **Feidhelm** (FAY·delm).

Fionn m. (FYUHN) From the Old Irish *finn* 'bright, fair'. In early Irish literature, and Irish and Scottish ballads and folktales, Finn mac Cumaill was a hero, poet and sometime outlaw who led a band of warriors known as the Fiana. The name was traditional in the O'Dempsey and O'Driscoll families. Anglicized as **Finn.**

Fionnabhair f. (fyuhn·OOR) From the Old Irish name Finnabarr: *finn* 'bright, fair' + *siabhre* 'phantom, fairy', the Irish equivalent of the Welsh Gwenhwyfar (Guenivere). A legendary Finnabarr was daughter of King Aillil and Queen Maeve of Connacht.

Fionnbharr m. (FYUHN·var) From the Old Irish *finn* 'bright, fair' + *barr* 'hair'. There are eight Irish saints by this name. The best-known is the 6th-century Saint Finnbarr, patron of Cork and of Barra in the Outer Hebrides, whose feast day is September 25. Currently a popular boys' name in Ireland. Anglicized as **Finbar.** Nicknames are **Barra** and **Bairre.**

Fionntán m. (FYUN·tawn) From the Old Irish *finn* 'bright, fair'. In myth, Fintan was the consort of Cessair, a woman who led the first wave of settlers to Ireland's shores. Fintan was the only one of this group who survived a great flood. Afterwards he lived on for thousands of years as a salmon, an eagle, and a hawk. Fintan was also the name of 74 early Irish saints.

Fionnuala f. (fi·NOO·a·la) From the Old Irish *finn* 'bright, fair' + *gúala* 'shoulders'. A popular name during the Middle Ages in the O'Brien, O'Connor and McDermott families, and later anglicized as **Finola** (fi·NOH·la); nickname **Nuala** (NOO·a·la).

Flann m. and f. (FLAHN) From the Old Irish *flann* 'blood red'. Flann has been the name of poets, scholars, abbots, saints, queens and kings. Flann Feórna was king of Kerry in the 8th century, and an ancestor of the O'Connors.

Gáeth m. (GAY) An Old Irish name meaning 'intelligent, skilful'.

Galvin m. (GAHL·vin) From the Old Irish *gelbann* 'a sparrow'.

Gearóid m. (GAHR·ohd) The Irish form of Gerald, introduced by the Anglo-Normans. A popular name.

Geiléis f. (GAY·lesh) From the Old Irish name Gelgéis: *gel* 'shining, bright' + *géis* 'swan'. The name of several early Irish princesses.

Gobnait f. (GOHB·nit) From the Old Irish *gobha* 'a smith'. The name of an early saint and abbess of Munster. One of her miracles was overcoming an army by unleashing her bees upon them. Gobnait's beehive, a holy relic, was kept for many years by the O'Herlihy family. Her feast day is February 11. Anglicized as **Gobnet.**

Gormlaith f. (GOORM·la) From the Old Irish *gorm* 'splendid' + *flaith* 'queen, sovereignty'. This name was especially popular in the Middle Ages, when it was borne by many queens, including the wife of Brian Boru. It is currently being revived as a woman's name, and is sometimes anglicized as **Gormley.**

Grania f. (GRAW·nya) From the Old Irish *gráinne* 'grain, seed'. This was probably the name of an ancient Irish grain goddess. In a famous medieval tale, Gráinne was betrothed to the hero Finn mac Cumhaill, but eloped with the irresistible Diarmaid instead. Grania Mhaol Ni Mhaolmhaigh (Grace O'Malley), a chieftainess of the Burkes of County Mayo, was renowned for her seafaring skill, and fought against the forces of Queen Elizabeth I. This is currently a popular name. Modern Irish **Gráinne** (GRAW·ne)

Isibéal f. (i·se·BEL) From the Norman French name Isabel.

Íte, Íde f. (EE·te) From the Old Irish *ite* 'thirst'. This saint's name is said to signify the thirst for divine love. The 6th-century Saint Íte was abbess of Killeedy in County Limerick. She composed a famous lullabye to the baby Jesus. Her feast day is January 15. Anglicized as **Ita.**

Jarlath m. (JAR·leth) The name of a 6th-century saint, the teacher of Saint Brendan the Navigator. Brendan told Jarlath to drive his chariot eastward and build a church wherever his wheel broke. Jarlath's wheel broke at Tuam, where he founded a church that became a great center of learning and art. His feast day is June 6. Modern Irish **Iarlaith** (YAHR·le).

Kennedy m. (KI·ne·dee) From the Old Irish name Cennétig: *cenn* 'head' + *étig* 'ugly'. Kennedy became a surname while continuing to be used as a first name. It was borne by Cennétig mac Lorcáin, father of high king Brian Boru.

Kilian m. (KIL·yan) From the Old Irish name Cilléne, perhaps from *cell* 'church'. Many saints bore this name, including an abbot of Iona in Scotland, whose feast day is July 3.

Laoire m. (LAY·re) From the Old Irish name Láegaire, which may mean 'calf-herder'. A popular name in early Ireland which was the name of two saints and a king of Tara. Anglicized as **Leary.**

Lasair f. (LOH·seer) From the Old Irish *lassa* 'flames'. This name was popular in early Ireland. Several queens and saints bore the name including Saint Lassar of Meath, whose feast day is February 18.

Lennán, Leannán m. (LAN·awn) An Old Irish word meaning 'lover, sweetheart'.

Líadan f. (LYAH·dan) An Old Irish name. Líadan was a poetess who was the beloved of the poet Cuirithur, although she was a nun. Another Líadan was mother of Saint Ciarán of Seir. She conceived him after swallowing a star that fell into her mouth as she lay sleeping.

Liam m. (LEE·am) The Irish form of William, short for Uilliam, which is derived from the name Guillaume, introduced in Ireland by the Anglo-Normans. Currently a popular name.

Lochlainn m. (LO*X*·lin) From the Old Irish word for the land of the Vikings. In Irish fairy tales, Lochlainn was the imaginary abode of the princess-who-must-be-rescued. This was a popular name in the early Middle Ages, especially in the MacTeague, MacCabe, Malone and MacCann families. Anglicized as **Loughlin.**

Lonán m. (LYO·nawn) From the Old Irish *lon* 'blackbird' + *-án,* the diminutive suffix. Eight early saints bore this name, including Saint Lonán Finn, whose feast day is January 22.

Lorcán m. (LOR·kawn) From the Old Irish *lorc* 'fierce' + *-án,* the diminutive suffix. Several early Irish kings bore the name Lorcán. Saint Lorcán Ó Tuathail (Laurence O'Toole), was Archbishop of

Dublin at the time of the Norman invasion. His feast day is November 14.

Lugh m. (LOO) The name of a Celtic god, from *lugu* 'light'. Lugh is also known as Lleu in Welsh myth. This has long been used as a personal name as well as the name of a deity. Nicknames include **Lughán** (LOO·awn) and **Lughna** (LOO·na).

Luíseach f. (LEE·sa*x*) A feminine form of Lugh, and the name of an early saint whose feast day is May 22.

Mac Dara m. (mahk·DAH·ra) From the Old Irish *mac* 'son' + *dara* 'oak'. Saint Mac Dara of Connemara is patron of fishermen. He is celebrated on two days, September 28 and July 16.

Macha f. (MAH·xa) Old Irish goddess name. Along with Badb and Morrígan, Macha was one of the three war goddesses of the Tuatha Dé Danaan. The name is associated with the royal site of Ulster, once known as Emain Macha (Twins of Macha), now Navan Fort, and with the nearby ecclesiastical site founded by Saint Patrick, Armagh (Ard Macha 'Hill of Macha'). A Saint Macha is patron of Killiney. Her feast day is February 6.

Maeve f. (MAYV) From the Old Irish name Medb 'intoxicating'. Medb Lethderg (Maeve of the Red Side) was a name of the goddess of sovereignty at Tara. She was said to have been the wife of nine successive kings, including Conn of the Hundred Battles, his son Art, and Art's son, Cormac mac Airt. Another Medb was the powerful queen of Connacht in the epic, *The Cattle Raid of Cooley*. This name is currently quite popular in Ireland. Modern Irish **Meadhbh.**

Máire f. (MAW·zhe, MAW·re) The Irish form of the name Mary. Irish girls were not named Máire before the 17th century; the name was considered too sacred. Instead, both girls and boys were given the name Maél Muire, meaning 'devotee of Mary'. Anglicized forms include **Moira, Maura** and **Maurya.**

Mairéad f. (MAW·rayt) From the Greek name meaning 'pearl'. This name became popular in Ireland due to admiration for Saint Margaret, who was queen of the Scots in the 11th century. **Peig** and **Peigí** are popular Irish-language nicknames for Mairéad.

Máirín f. (maw·ZHEEN, maw·REEN) A diminutive of Máire, and also a popular name in its own right. Also written **Maureen.**

Malachy m. (MA·la·kee) A Hebrew name, widely used in Ireland as an anglicization for Irish names that begin with *máel* 'servant or devotee' such as Máel Máedóc and Máel Sechlainn. Saint Malachy of Armagh was a church reformer of the 12th century. His feast day is November 3.

Manus m. (MA·nuhs) From the Latin *magnus* 'great'. This name was borrowed from the Norse, who in turn borrowed it from Carolus Magnus, the Latin name of the French Emperor Charlemagne. The name has been popular since the early Middle Ages.

Marcán m. (MOR·kawn) From the Old Irish *marc* 'horse' + the diminutive *-án*. Marcán mac Cennétig, the brother of High King Brian Boru, was abbot of Killaloe. Saint Marcán of Clonenagh has a feast day of October 21.

Margo f. (MOHR·gaw) In legend, Margo was a fairy and the mother of the beautiful Étain.

Mathghamhain m. (ma·HOHN) An Old Irish word for 'bear' and a popular man's name during the Middle Ages, borne by a brother of High King Brian Boru. It was traditional in the O'Connor, O'Brien and O'Farrell families. Anglicized as **Mahon.**

Meallán m. (MAHL·an) From the Old Irish *mall* 'lightning' + *-án*, the diminutive suffix. Three early saints by this name have feast days of January 28, February 7 and October 26.

Mell, Mella f. (MAHL, MAH·la) From the Old Irish *mall* 'lightning'. Mell, the sister of Saint Kevin, was the mother of seven saints.

Mícheál m. (MEE·xal) The Irish form of Michael.

Miles, Myles m. Several derivations have been suggested for this name, including the Latin *miles* 'soldier'. It is worth noting that the last prehistoric invasion of Ireland, according to legend, was that of the Sons of Mil. Miles is a traditional name in Ireland for the same reason as Malachy: from the 17th century onwards, it was used to anglicize many of the traditional Irish names that begin with *máel* 'servant or devotee', such as Máel Muire and Máel Mórda.

Mona f. (MOH·na) From the old Irish name Muadnat, derived from *muad* 'noble, good'. Saint Muadnat of Drumcliffe has a feast day of January 6. Modern Irish **Muadhnait** (MOO·uh·nit).

Mór f. (MOHR) From the Old Irish *mór* 'great, tall'. Until the 19th century, Mór was one of the most popular Irish women's names. A diminutive is **Móirín,** anglicized as **Moreen.**

Morann m. (MOOR·an) From the Old Irish name, Morand, the derivation of which is uncertain. Morand was a legendary judge of ancient Ireland who reputedly never gave a false verdict. The name was borne by several of Finn mac Cumhaill's warriors.

Muireann f. (MEER·an) From the Old Irish *muir* 'sea'. In tales of Finn mac Cumaill, Muireann was the wife of Finn's son, Oisín. Another legendary Queen Muireann was ancestress of the kings of Connacht. Four abbesses of Kildare also bore this very popular early name.

Muirín f. (MEER·een) From the Old Irish *muir* 'sea' + *gein* 'birth'. In the 6th century, a 300-year-old pagan mermaid by this name was captured in Lough Neagh by the fisherman of Saint Comgall. Comgall baptized her, enabling her to go to heaven.

Muiríol f. (MEER·ol) From the Old Irish name Muirgel: *muir* 'sea' + *gel* 'bright, shining'. Muriol was the name of several early queens of Leinster.

Muiríos m. (MEER·ees) From the Old Irish name Muirgius: *muir* 'sea' + *gus* 'strength, vigor'. Muiríos was the name of several kings of Connacht, and was traditional among the McDonaghs and McDermotts.

Muirne f. (MEER·ne) An ancient name that may mean high-spirited. Muirne Muncháem (Lovely-Shouldered Muirne) was the mother of Finn mac Cumaill. Also written **Myrna, Morna.**

Murchadh m. (MOOR·uh·xa) From the Old Irish *muir* 'sea' + *cath* 'warrior'. The name of several early kings and warriors, favored by the O'Brien, O'Flaherty, O'Connell and O'Donovan families.

Nessa f. (NES·a) f. An Old Irish name. Nessa was the name of the mother of Conchobar mac Nessa, the great legendary king of

Ulster. According to an early tale, she was originally named Assa, which means 'gentle', until one day she came home and found that her twelve foster fathers had been murdered by an outlaw band. She became a woman warrior to avenge their deaths, and changed her name to Ni-assa 'ungentle', or Nessa.

Niall m. (NEE·al) An Old Irish name which may be derived from *nél* 'cloud'. One of the most famous legendary kings of Tara was Niall Noígiallach (Niall of the Nine Hostages). He founded the Uí Neill dynasty, and was the ancestor of both the Irish O'Neills and the Scottish MacNeils. Niall became king after agreeing to kiss a hag, who then turned into a beautiful woman—the goddess of sovereignty, in fact. She then conferred kingship upon him. The name Niall was traditional in the O'Neill, O'Donnell, O'Higgins, O'Quinn, O'Kelly, O'Boyle, and O'Doherty families. Niall is currently a popular boys' name in Ireland. Nickname: **Niallán** (NEE·a·lahn).

Niamh f. (NEE·av) From an Old Irish name Niam, meaning 'luster, sheen, brilliance'. Several legendary women bore this name. One was a princess of Tir-na-n'Og (the Land of Youth), who took Finn mac Cumhaill's son Oisín to the otherworld. This name is currently quite popular in Ireland. It is also written **Niam.** The Welsh version of the name is **Nia.**

Nora, Norah f. (NOH·ra) An Irish version of the Latin name, Honora. A classic Irish woman's name.

Oisín m. (oh·SHEEN) From the Old Irish *oisín* 'fawn'. Oisín, the son of the legendary hero Finn mac Cumaill, was the poet of the Fiana. Two saints by this name (Oissíne) have feast days of January 1 and May 1. This is currently a popular name.

Órán m. (OHR·an) From *odrán,* the Old Irish word for 'otter'. Saint Odrán is patron of Waterford. His feast day is May 8.

Órla f. (OHR·la) From the Old Irish *ór* 'gold' + *flaith* 'sovereignty, queen'. This name is closely associated with the high king Brian Boru, having been the name of his sister and his daughter. The name was popular in the Middle Ages, and is becoming popular again today. Modern Irish **Órlaith.**

Oscar m. (OHS·kar) From the Old Irish *os* 'deer', perhaps meaning 'one who loves deer'. Oscar was a legendary warrior, grandson of Finn mac Cumaill. The name was traditional in the MacLoughlin, Maguire and O'Connor families.

Pádraig m. (PAH·drig) From the Latin name Patricius 'noble'. Saint Patrick, patron saint of Ireland, was the first successful Christian missionary to the island. The name Patrick has only been given to children in Ireland since about the year 1700. Earlier, it had been considered too sacred, and children were given the names Gilla Pátraic (servant of Patrick) or Máel Pátraic (devotee of Patrick) instead. Saint Patrick's feast day is March 17.

Pádraigin f. (PAH·dri·geen) A recent feminine form of Pádraig.

Piaras m. (PEER·as) An Irish form of Peter, from the Norman French name Piers. Anglicized as **Pierce.**

Réamonn m. (RAY·moon) The Irish form of Raymond.

Rían m. (REE·an) A diminutive of the Old Irish *rí* 'king'. This old first name is the source of the surname Ryan, which has been adopted as a first name in North America. A related name from early Ireland is **Rígán,** also pronounced REE·an.

Riocard m. (REE·kard) The Irish form of Richard, introduced by the Anglo-Normans.

Ríonach f. (REE·uh·na*x*) From the Old Irish name Rígnach 'queenly'. A Queen Ríonach was the legendary ancestress of the O'Neills, MacLoughlins, O'Donnells, O'Gallaghers and O'Gormleys. Also written **Riona.**

Ríordán m. (REER·dawn) From Old Irish *rígbarddán* 'royal poet'.

Rónán m. (ROH·nawn) From the Old Irish *rón* 'seal' + the diminutive suffix *-án*. Ten saints bore this name, including Rónán of Lough Derg, whose feast day is January 13, and Rónán of Lismore, whose feast day February 9.

Rós f. (ROHS) The derivation of this name is uncertain: it may be either from the Germanic *hros* 'horse' or the English 'rose'. Rós has been a traditional name among the O'Kanes and O'Murrays. A popular nickname is **Róisín** (row·SHEEN).

Ross m. (RAWS) Old Irish *ros* 'promontory'. This has been a popular name since earliest historical times, borne by kings, heroes and saints, and a traditional name among the Coughlins, O'Farrells and MacMahons. Ross MacMahon, Archbishop of Armagh, was an opponent of Cromwell.

Rúadán m. (ROO·an) From the Old Irish *rúad* 'red-haired'. The 6th-century Saint Rúadán, Abbot of Lorrha, has a feast day of April 15.

Ruarc m. (ROO·ark) From the Old Irish *arg* 'champion, hero', and the source of the surname, O'Rourke. Anglicized as **Rourke.**

Ruairí m. (ROO·e·ree) From the Old Irish name Ruaidrí: *rúad* 'red' + *rí* 'king'. The last high king of Ireland, Ruaidri Ua Conchobair, died in 1170. The name was traditional among the O'Connors, O'Shaughnessys, MacDonnells, MacCanns, McGinleys, Mulloys and O'Donnells. Anglicized as **Rory.**

Sadhbh f. (SAH·eev) From the Old Irish name Sadb, which may mean 'sweet' or 'goodness'. Sadhbh was the name of several real and legendary Irish princesses, including the daughters of Conn of the Hundred Battles, of Queen Medb of Connacht, and of King Brian Boru. Also written **Sabha** (SE·va).

Saorla f. (SAYR·la) From the Old Irish name Sáerlaith: *sáer* 'noble' + *flaith* 'queen, sovereignty'.

Scáthach f. (SKAW·hak) From the Old Irish *scáth* 'shadow, shade'. Scáthach was a legendary woman warrior and prophetess who gave final battle training to the Ulster hero Cú Chulainn.

Séafra m. (SHE·fra) The Irish form of Geoffrey or Jeffrey.

Séamus m. (SHAY·muhs) The Irish form of James.

Seán m. (SHAWN) The Irish form of John, derived from the Norman French name, Jehan. Also written **Shaun, Shawn** and **Shane.**

Séanait f. (SHAY·nat) From the Old Irish name Ségnat, derived from *séig* 'a hawk'.

Seanán m. (SHAW·nawn) From the Old Irish *sen* 'ancient'. Seanán was the name of twenty early Irish saints, including Saint Senán of Iniscathy, whose feast day is March 8.

Shannon f. (SHAH·non) The name of the longest river in Ireland, which takes its name from the old Irish goddess Sinann, granddaughter of Manannán Mac Lir. Shannon is not used as a first name in Ireland.

Síle f. (SHEE·la) The Irish form of Cecilia. Also written **Sheila.**

Sinéad f. (shi·NAYD) An Irish version of the Norman French name Jonet. Another is **Sine** (SHEE·na).

Siobhán f. (shi·VAWN) From the Norman French name, Jehanne, a feminine form of Jehan (the equivalent of the English John). A nickname is **Siobhánín** (shi·VAWN·een).

Síomha f. (SHEE·va) From the Old Irish name Síthmaith: *síth* 'peace' + *maith* 'good'. Síthmaith was the name of an 8th-century abbess of Clonburren. Anglicized as **Sheeva.**

Sláine f. (SLAH·nye) This name was used in medieval times by the MacNamaras and O'Briens. Anglicized as **Slany.**

Sléibhín m. (SLE·veen) From the Old Irish *sleib* 'mountain', meaning 'mountain man'. A Saint Slébíne was abbot of Iona in Scotland in the 8th century. His feast day is March 2.

Sorcha f. (SOO·ruh·xa) From the Old Irish *sorchae* 'bright, radiant'. Sorcha has been a popular woman's name in Ireland from the Middle Ages to the present day.

Suibhne m. (SHEEV·ne) From the Old Irish name Suibne, borne by several early saints and kings. King Suibne Gelt (Mad Sweeney) went insane in the battle of Mag Rath in 637 as the result of a curse laid on him by a saint he had insulted. He spent the rest of his life living in the trees and composing nature poetry. Anglicized as **Sweeney.**

Tara f. (TAH·ra) From the Old Irish name Temair. In legend, Teamair was the wife of Érémon, leader of the ancestors of the Irish, the Sons of Mil. Teamair gave her name to the hill of Tara, traditional seat of Irish kingship. Modern Irish **Teamhair** (TOHR).

Tárlach m. (TAHR·lax) From the Old Irish name Tairdelbach, which means 'one who assists or aids'. This was a popular name during the Middle Ages. Two kings by this name were Tairdelbach, King of Munster, and Tairdelbach Ó Connor, King of Ireland. This was a traditional name among the O'Connors, O'Briens, O'Donnells, O'Boyles and MacSweeneys. Anglicized as **Turlough.**

Tiarnach m. (TEER·nah*x*) From the Old Irish name Tigernach, from *tigerna* 'lord, superior, chief'. This was the name of several saints, including Saint Tigernach of Clones, whose feast day is April 4. Anglicized as **Tierney.**

Tiarnán m. (TEER·nawn) From the Old Irish name Tigernán: *tigerna* 'lord, superior, chief' + the diminutive *-án.* A popular name in early and medieval Ireland, and was borne by several kings and saints, including Saint Tigernán of County Mayo, whose feast day is April 8. It was a traditional name among the O'Rourkes, MacGoverns and MacKiernans. Anglicized as **Tiernan.**

Treasach m. (TRAH·sa*x*) From the Old Irish name Tressach, meaning 'fierce, warlike.' Anglicized as **Tracy.**

Tyrone m. (teer·OHN) From the Old Irish *tir* 'land' + *Eoghain* 'of Eoghán' (a man's name). Tyrone is the name of a county in Northern Ireland and is also used as a first name.

Úna f. (OO·na) From the Old Irish *úan* 'lamb'. In legend, Úna was a daughter of a king of Lochlainn. The name was very popular in Ireland the Middle Ages. Also written **Oona, Oonagh.**

WALES

The *Cymry Cymraeg*—Welsh-speaking Welsh—have been giving their children the traditional names of the Middle Ages for at least two generations. Today, if you walk the streets of nearly any town in Wales you will run into Ceridwens, Peredurs, Morfudds, Rhyses, and more Geraints than you can shake a stick at. Even those who speak little or no Welsh have returned to the old names in order to reclaim their cultural heritage and express their individuality.

The Welsh language has flourished on the island of Britain for over 2,000 years. When the Romans conquered the region in 43 AD, the British tongue, ancestor language of Welsh, was spoken throughout the southern half of the island. The Celtic upper classes seem to have learned Latin for official purposes while continuing to speak British amongst themselves. Very little British writing remains from this period aside from inscriptions on coins, buildings, statues and votive tablets, and most of the words we know from this period are the names of men and women, gods and goddesses.

Some literature in Old Welsh has survived from the period before 1150, most notably the poetry of Aneurin and Taliesin, which was probably composed in the 6th century. At that time, a language very similar to Welsh was spoken in the area that is now northwestern England and southern Scotland, a land known in Welsh as *Yr Hen Ogledd* (the Old North). This was the location of the battle of Gododdin, immortalized in an old Welsh poem of the same name. Early Welsh oral and literary tradition is preserved in manuscripts from the 12th to 16th centuries. The content of these is much older than the manuscripts themselves, since important works of history and literature were copied again and again. Rare and valuable books of old knowledge such as the Red Book of Hergest and the the White Book of Rhydderch were privately owned until a century ago. These works contain the celebrated *Mabinogi,* a collection of mythological tales. Other early Welsh literature in medieval manuscripts includes tales of King Arthur, and large quantities of poetry and history.

The translation of the Bible into Welsh in the late 16th century marks the beginning of Modern Welsh. Today, around half a million people speak Welsh, and the study and use of the language is supported in schools, libraries, universities, publishing, radio and television. Most of the differences between Middle and Modern Welsh are in grammar rather than vocabulary, so that the words that form the basis of many older names are easily understood by Welsh speakers today.

Throughout the Middle Ages and Renaissance, most people in Wales either gave their children Welsh names or adopted popular English and French names with a strong Welsh accent. The Catholic Church encouraged people to name their children after saints, and there were more than enough saints with Welsh names from which to choose. This situation changed in the 17th century when evangelical religious revivals led to the establishment of the Methodist and Baptist churches in Wales. Many who belonged to these churches felt that they should give their children names from the Bible, so that by the mid-18th century it seemed that every other person in Wales was named John or Mary. This movement away from Welsh names soon reversed, however.

Since middle of the 19th century, the National Eisteddfod, an annual festival of poetry and music, has served to perpetuate and encourage the Welsh language. The Eisteddfod is sponsored by the Gorsedd of the Bards, an organization of poets and scholars. A person inducted into the Gorsedd adopts a Welsh 'bardic' name. They may choose a name with historical resonance, like Talhearn (Iron Brow); Emrys, one of Merlin's names; or Caradog, the name of an ancient Celtic ruler who rebelled against the Romans. Some transliterate their English names into Welsh, as did Ioan Siencyn (John Jenkins), or choose a metaphorical name, like Ellis Evans, who wrote under the pen name Hedd Wyn, meaning 'holy peace'. The tradition of bardic names has brought many older names back into use.

The translation of the *Mabinogi* and other early literary works into English has been another means of keeping these traditional names names alive. By the 20th century, the names of mythological and legendary characters like Rhiannon, Ceridwen and Geraint had become quite fashionable. Pan-Celtic solidarity has resulted in the popularity of Welsh names based on Irish names such as Ethni, from the Irish Eithne, and Nia, from the Irish Niamh.

From before the Roman conquest until the 18th century, a Welsh person was known by two names: a personal name plus the father's name. A man named Rhys whose father's name was Tewdur would be known as Rhys ap Tewdur. *Ap* or *ab* is a contraction of the word *map* or *mab* meaning 'son, boy'. A woman might be known as Nest verch Rhys, *verch* or *merch* signifying 'daughter, girl'. Welsh women did not change their names upon marriage. In a few cases, mostly in myth and legend, a person was known as the child of their mother, as were Mabon ap Modron and Arianrhod verch Dôn.

In the 18th century, when the English began to exploit the coal and other natural resources of Wales, industrialists insisted that their Welsh employees adopt hereditary surnames. Most changed their *ap* name to a permanent family name. Ap Rhys was contracted to Price, ap Evan to Bevan. Some individuals added *-s* to the patronymic, as did the children of John, who became the ubiquitous Joneses.

Believe it or not, Welsh spelling is completely phonetic. Basically, if a letter is there, you pronounce it. The letter *w* is a vowel and is pronounced 'oo'. The letter *y* is more or less an 'uh', unless it is in the last syllable of a word, in which case it's an 'ee'. The three Welsh letter combinations that cause outsiders the most difficulty are *ll*, *rh* and *dd*. Simplest first: *dd* is pronounced like the *th* in the English word 'this'. The notorious *ll* and *rh* are breathy versions of *l* and *r*. To pronounce *ll*, place your tongue as though you were going to make an American 'l' then breathe out a short, sharp breath. Likewise for *rh:* position your tongue as for a Spanish *r*, and make the same short, sharp breath. The pronunciations in the list below reflect the way a Welsh speaker without a very strong local accent would pronounce the name. Unless noted otherwise, the meanings given for each name are from Middle Welsh.

Angharad f. (ahng·HAHR·ahd) From the Welsh *an-*, an intensifying prefix + *caru* 'love'. This name was very popular in the Middle Ages, and is still considered a classic Welsh woman's name. The legendary Angharad Ton Velen (Angharad Yellow Wave, perhaps a reference to her hair) was noted for her liveliness.

Arianell f. (ah·ree·AHN·e*lh*) From Welsh *arian* 'silver'.

Arianrhod, Aranrhod f. (ah·ree·AHN·*rh*od, ah·RAHN·*rh*od) From Welsh *arian* 'silver' + *rhod* 'wheel, circle, orbit'. In the *Mabinogi,* Arianrhod verch Dôn was the mother of Dylan eil Tôn and Llew Llaw Gyffes.

Arianwen, Aranwen f. (ah·ree·AHN·wen, ah·RAHN·wen) From Welsh *arian* 'silver' + *gwen* 'shining, holy'.

Arianwyn m. (ah·ree·AHN·win) From Welsh *arian* 'silver' + *gwyn* 'shining, holy'.

Arthur m. (AHR·thir) From Celtic **artos* 'bear', or possibly from the Latin name Artorius (also from an Indo-European bear word). This was the name of the legendary king and culture hero of the Welsh, Cornish and Bretons.

Auron f. (AYR·on) From Welsh *aur* 'gold' + *-on,* a divine ending. Also written **Euron.**

Barri m. (BAHR·ee) Probably from Welsh *bar* 'mound, summit, dune'. The island of Barry off the Glamorgan coast is named for a 6th-century hermit, Saint Barri, who took refuge there. After his death the island became a popular pilgrimage destination. Saint Barri's feast day is September 27.

Bethan f. (BETH·ahn) One of the most popular Welsh nicknames for Elizabeth. Others are **Bet, Beti, Betsan** and **Betsi.**

Bleddyn m. (BLE*TH*·in) From Welsh *blaidd* 'wolf' + *-yn,* a diminutive suffix. Wolf was an epithet used for warriors and outlaws. Other

Welsh wolf names include **Bledri** (BLED·ree): *blaidd* + *rhi* 'king' and **Bleiddian** (BLAY*TH*·yahn): *blaidd* + *-ian,* a verbal ending, 'one who goes wolfing, *i.e.,* looting, raiding'.

Blodeuwedd f. (blod·AY·we*th*) From Welsh *blodau* 'flowers' + *gwedd* 'appearance, form'. In the *Mabinogi,* Blodeuwedd was the wife of Llew Llaw Gyffes. The magicians Gwydion and Math made her out of the flowers of oak, broom and meadow-sweet, and when she refused to do their bidding, they changed her into an owl.

Blodwen f. (BLOD·wen) From *blodyn* 'flower' + *gwen* 'shining, holy'. Blodwen is one of the classic Welsh girls' names. Flowers and other natural objects are very popular as personal names in Wales, especially for girls.

Brân m. (BRAN) The Welsh word for 'crow'. The most famous bearer of this name was Brân Bendigeidfran (Brân the Blessed) in the Second Branch of the *Mabinogi.*

Branwen f. (BRAN·wen) From Welsh *bran* 'crow' + *gwen* 'shining, holy'. In the *Mabinogi,* Branwen is the sister of Brân. They are the male and female aspects of the Celtic war deity. Branwen is a popular name in Wales

Briallen f. (bree·*ALH*·en) From Welsh *briallu* 'primrose'. A popular flower name.

Bronwen f. (BRON·wen) From Welsh *bron* 'breast' + *gwen* 'shining, holy'.

Bryn m. (BRIN) The Welsh word for 'hill'. Bryn is one of the most popular Welsh boys' names. **Brynley** and **Brinley** (BRIN·lee), two names derived from Bryn, are popular as well.

Cadeyrn m. (KAHD·ayrn) From Welsh *cad* 'battle' + *teyrn* 'prince'.

Cadfan m. (KAHD·vahn) From Welsh *cad* 'battle' + *ban* 'summit'. A 6th-century saint by this name is associated with a healing well. His feast day is November 1.

Cadoc m. (KAHD·ok) From the Welsh *cad* 'battle'. Originally a nickname for **Cadfael** (KAHD·vil) from *cad* 'battle' + *mael* 'prince'. Cadoc was the name of one of the most important early Welsh saints. According to an early account of his life, Saint Cadoc was carried on a cloud to Northern Italy, where he became a bishop and was martyred. His feast day is January 24.

Cadwaladr m. (kahd·WAHL·ah·der) From Welsh *cad* 'battle' + *gwaladr* 'ruler, leader'. Cadwaladr was a 7th-century saint and ruler of the northern kingdom of Gwynedd. His feast day is October 9.

Caerwyn m. (KIR·win or KAYR·win) From Welsh *caer* 'fort' + *gwyn* 'shining, holy'.

Cai, Cei m. (KAY) Usually derived from the Latin name Caius, but possibly cognate with Irish *cái (cói)* 'path, way'. Cai was described as King Arthur's closest companion from his earliest appearance in Welsh literature. According to a 10th-century poem, *Pa gur yw y porthawr,* Cai killed nine witches and rid the island of Anglesey of a fierce monster called the Palug Cat.

Cari f. (KAHR·ee) From Welsh *caru* 'to love'. Other women's names from this root are **Caryl** (KAHR·il) and **Carys** (KAHR·ees).

Catrin f. (KAHT·reen) The Welsh form of Catherine. Catrin of Berain (1534–1591) was called the 'Mother of Wales' because she had so many important descendants. Nicknames for Catrin include **Cati** (KAHT·ee) and **Cadi** (KAHD·ee).

Celyn m. (KEL·in) The Welsh word for 'holly'. Celyn ap Caw was a member of Arthur's court in the medieval tale, *Kulhwch and Olwen.*

Ceri m. & f. (KER·ee) The name of two rivers, one in Dyfed and one in Glamorgan. The name may come from Welsh *caru* 'to love'. A very popular name.

Ceridwen f. (ker·ID·wen) Possibly from Welsh *cerdd* 'song' + *gwen* 'shining, holy'; or from *cariad* 'beloved' + *gwen* 'shining, holy'. Ceridwen was a powerful sorceress in the tale of Taliesin.

Cian m. (KEE·an) Possibly from Welsh *ci (cwn)* 'hound, wolf', or from the Old Irish *cian* 'ancient, enduring'. Cian is known as one of the five Cynfeirdd, the founding poets of the Welsh tradition, although none of his poems has survived.

Collen m. (KOLH·en) The Welsh word for 'hazel tree'. The name of a 6th-century saint, whose feast day is May 21.

Cynan m. (KUHN·ahn) From Celtic **kuno* 'great, high'. A popular name in medieval Wales. Cynan Garwyn was a 6th-century ruler of Powys. One of the earliest Welsh poems, *Trawsganu Cynan Garwyn mab Brochfael,* is a eulogy listing the many famous battles won by Cynan and his ancestors, and the generous gifts they gave their poets.

Dafydd m. (DAH·vi*th*) The Welsh form of David. Saint David is the patron saint of Wales. His feast day is March 1. The popularity of the name in Wales is reflected in the number of its nicknames: **Dafi** (DAH-vee), **Dai** (DII), **Deian** (DAY-an), **Deio** (DAY-oh), and most especially **Dewi** (DE-wee).

Daron f. (DAHR·on) From Welsh *dàr* 'oak' + *-on,* a divine ending. The name of an oak goddess and of a river in Caernarvonshire.

Deiniol m. (DAYN·yol) The Welsh form of Daniel. Saint Deiniol was active in the late 6th century in North Wales. His feast day is September 11.

Del, Delyth f. (DEL, DEL·ith) From Welsh *del* 'pretty'.

Dilys f. (DIL·ees) From Welsh *dilys* 'genuine'. A genuinely popular name that originated in the 19th century.

Dôn, Dona f. (DOHN, DOHN·ah) This was the name of a mother goddess in Welsh mythology, cognate to the Irish Danu. The Celtic root of her name shows up in river names across Europe, including the Danube and the Don.

Dwyn, Dwynwen f. (DWIN, DWIN·wen) From Welsh *dwyn* 'pleasant, agreeable' + *gwen* 'shining, holy'. Saint Dwynwen lived in the 5th century. Women traditionally prayed to her either for help finding sweethearts, or for help in becoming indifferent to them afterwards. Dwynwen's feast day is January 25.

Dylan m. (DUHL·an) A Welsh word for 'ocean, sea, the deep'. In the *Mabinogi,* Dylan eil Tôn (Sea Like a Wave) was the name of a son of Aranrhod. Welsh-born Dylan Thomas was one of the finest English language poets of the 20th century.

Eira, Eiry f. (AY·rah, AY·ree) From Welsh *eira* 'snow'.

Eirianwen f. (ayr·YAHN·wen) From Welsh *eirian* 'splendid, bright, fair' + *gwen* 'shining, holy'.

Eiriol, Eirlys f. (AYR·yol, AYR·lees) From Welsh *eira* 'snow'. Both are names for the flower 'snowdrop'.

Eleri f. (el·AYR·ee) This name may derive from Welsh *el-* 'greatly, much' + *geri* 'bitter'. Eleri is the name of a river in Ceredigion and of a 5th-century saint. A popular name.

Elis m. (EL·is) The Welsh form of Elijah, by way of Greek Elias. One of the most consistently popular names for Welsh men over the years. Also spelled **Ellis** (E*LH*·is).

Eluned, Luned (el·EEN·ed, LEEN·ed) From Welsh *el-* 'greatly, much' + **(i)uned* 'wish, desire'. Luned was the handmaiden of the Lady of the Fountain in the Welsh Arthurian romance *Owein.* She had a magic ring that made the wearer invisible—one of the Thirteen Treasures of the Island of Britain. Eluned's beauty and intelligence were legendary.

Emlyn m. (EM·lin) From Latin *aemilianus* 'flattering, charming'.

Emrys m. (EM·rees) From the Latin name Ambrosius. Emrys was an epithet of the magician and poet Myrddin (Merlin).

Enfys f. (EN·vees) The Welsh word for 'rainbow', and currently a popular name.

Enid f. (EE·nid) From Breton *Bro Wened,* a territory corresponding to the area around modern-day Vannes in Brittany. Enid verch Niwl Iarll (Daughter of the Earl of the Mist) is the heroine of a Welsh Arthurian romance, *Geraint mab Erbin.* She may originally have been a Celtic goddess of sovereignty, an embodiment of the land, to whom any true king must be symbolically married.

Essyllt f. (ES·i*lh*t) From the British **adsiltia* 'she who is gazed at'. The Welsh form of Isolde, the tragic heroine of the Tristan saga.

Evan m. (EV·ahn) A Welsh form of John. Other forms include **Ioan** (YOH·ahn), **Ianto** (YAHN·toh), **Iwan** (YEW·ahn) and **Ieuan** (YAY·ahn).

Ffion, Ffiona f. (FEE·on, fee·OH·nah) From *ffion* 'foxglove'. This is a very popular name.

Fflur f. (FLEER) The Welsh word for 'flower'. In a medieval legend, Julius Caesar kidnapped the beautiful Fflur from Britain and took her to Rome. Her sweetheart Caswallon, disguised as a shoemaker, followed and won her back.

Ffraid f. (FRAYD) The Welsh form of Brigid, the Irish saint. Her feast day is February 1.

Ffransis m. (FRAWN·sis) The Welsh form of Francis. The nickname Frank is **Ffranc** in Welsh.

Gaenor, Gaynor f. (GAY·nor) A form of Gwenhwyfar (Guenivere) and a very popular name in the 19th and early 20th centuries.

Gareth m. (GAHR·eth) From Welsh *gwaraidd* 'civilized'. Tennyson used this name for one of King Arthur's knights in his *Idylls of the King*.

Geraint m. (GER-iint) From Celtic *Gerontios,* cognate with Greek *gerontius* 'old'. Geraint mab Erbin was the hero of a medieval Welsh romance. He was a knight of the Round Table, renowned for his prowess in tournaments, and won his wife Enid in this way. He was also said to have been king of Cornwall. A Welsh elegy to Geraint mab Erbin dates from around 900, and he is also mentioned as one of the warriors in the *Gododdin*. Geraint is one of the most popular names in Wales.

Gerallt m. (GER·a*l*ht) The Welsh form of Gerald. Gerald of Wales, also known as Giraldus Cambrensis and Gerallt Gymro (1146–1223) was a half-Welsh half-Norman cleric who wrote several works on the Celtic realms in the late 12th century.

Gethin m. (GETH-in) From Welsh *cethin* 'dark, dusky'.

Gildas m. (GIL-dahs) The 6th-century monk and saint Gildas was the author of *De excidio Britanniae* (The Destruction of Britain) a rabble-rousing work in which he blamed his fellow Welsh for allowing the Anglo-Saxons to overrun Britain. Saint Gildas is venerated in Brittany as Saint Gweltas, and he is credited there with performing numerous miracles. His feast day is January 29.

Gladys, Gwladys f. (GLAH·dis, goo·LAH·dis) From Welsh *gwlad* 'land, nation, sovereignty'.

Glenys f. (GLEN·is) From Welsh *glan* 'riverbank, shore'.

Glyn m. (GLIN) From Welsh *glyn* 'valley'. A very popular name.

Glynis, Glynys f. (GLIN·is) From Welsh *glyn* 'valley'. The feminine form of Glyn.

Goronwy m. (gohr·ON·wee) From Welsh *gwr* 'man'. Goronwy Owen (1723–1769) was a great poet of the 18th-century Welsh language renaissance. He emigrated to the colonies and died in Virginia. Variants are **Goronw** (gohr·ON·oo) and **Gronw** (GROHN·oo). In the *Mabinogi*, Gronw Pebyr (Gronw the Radiant) was the chosen lover of Blodeuwedd.

Griffith, Gruffudd, Gruffydd m. (GRIF·*ith*) From Welsh *cryf* 'strong' + udd 'lord'. A classic Welsh man's name. Many medieval rulers of Wales were named Gruffudd.

Gwawr f. (GWOWR) A Welsh word for 'dawn'. The name has become popular in recent years.

Gwen (GWEN) f., **Gwyn** (GWIN) m. From Welsh *gwen, gwyn* 'white, shining, holy'; ultimately from Celtic and Indo-European roots referring to shiningness as light, sight, perception, discovery. Brightness is associated with the Celtic otherworld. In Welsh myth, Gwyn ap Nudd was the leader of the Wild Hunt and the lord of lost souls.

Gwenda f. (GWEN·dah) From Welsh *gwen* 'shining, holy' + *da* 'good'.

Gwendolen f. (gwen·DOHL·en) From Welsh *gwen* 'shining, holy' + *dolen* 'link'.

Gwenhwyfar f. (gwen·HWIV·ahr) The Welsh original of the name Guenivere, from *gwen* 'shining, holy' + *hwyfar* 'phantom, spirit, fairy'. Gwenhwyfar was one of the most common names among Welsh women from the Middle Ages until the 19th century, especially in North Wales.

Gwenith f. (GWEN·ith) The Welsh word for 'wheat'.

Gwenllian, Gwenlliant f. (gwen·*LHEE*·ahn, gwen·*LHEE*·ahnt) From Welsh *gwen* 'shining, holy' + *lliant* 'stream'. Gwenllian has been a popular Welsh name since the Middle Ages.

Gwenno f. (GWEN·oh) A nickname for Gwen names.

Gwerfyl, Gwerful f. (GWAYR·vil) Gwerful Mechain was a poet of 15th-century Powys, one of the few early Welsh women poets whose work has been preserved.

Gwilym m. (GWIL·im) The Welsh form of William.

Gwyddno m. (GWI*TH*·noh) From Welsh *gwyd* 'knowledge' + *gno* 'fame'. Gwyddno Garanhir (Gwyddno Long-Leg or Tall Crane) owned one of the Thirteen Treasures of the Island of Britain, a magical hamper. When food for one person was put in it, food for a hundred would be found when the hamper was opened.

Gwydion m. (GWID·yon) From Welsh *gwyd* 'knowledge' + *-on,* a divine ending. Gwydion ap Dôn was a powerful magician in the *Mabinogi.* In Welsh, *Caer Gwydion* (Gwydion's Castle) is the Milky Way.

Gwyneira m. (gwin·AYR·ah) From Welsh *gwyn* 'shining, holy' + *eira* 'snow'.

Gwyneth f. (GWIN·eth) From Welsh *gwen* 'shining, holy' + *geneth* 'girl', or from *gwynaeth* 'happiness, bliss'.

Hafgan m. and f. (HAHV·gahn) From Welsh *haf* 'summer' + *cân* 'song'.

Hafren f. (HAHV-ren) From the Celtic name Sabrina, the goddess of the river Severn.

Heddwyn m. (HE*TH*·win) From Welsh *hedd* 'peace' + *gwyn* 'shining, holy'. Hedd Wyn was the bardic name of Ellis Evans (1887–1917), a poet and soldier killed in Flanders during World War I, who posthumously won the chair at the 1917 Eisteddfod. His life has become a symbol of the futility of war.

Heledd f. (HEL·e*th*) From Welsh *hy-*, a particle indicating goodness + *ledd* 'wound'. Heledd was a legendary poetess of early Wales, the sister of Cynddylan ap Cyndrwn. The poems attributed to Heledd lament her brother's death and the destruction of his household. Because of the theme of homelessness in her poetry, Heledd was known as one of the Three Wanderers of Arthur's Court.

Heulwen f. (HIIL·wen) From Welsh *heul* 'sun' + *gwen* 'shining, holy'. Other sun-names are **Heulfryn** (HIIL·vrin) *heul* + *bryn* 'hill', a male name, and **Heulyn** (HIIL·een) 'ray of sunshine', which can be either masculine or feminine.

Huw m. (HYOO) The Welsh version of Hugh, from Old German *hugi* 'intelligence, spirit'. A perennially popular Welsh name.

Hywel m. (HUH·wel) From Welsh *hywel* 'eminent'. Hywel Dda (Hywel the Good) was a king of Wales in the 10th century. He collected the oral legal tradition, passed down from the druids, and made it into a written code of law. Anglicized as Howell.

Hywela f. (huh·WEL·ah) Feminine form of Hywel.

Ieuan m. (YAY·an) From the Latin name Johannes. Ieuan is a Welsh equivalent of the English name John. Others are **Ioan** (YOH·an), **Iwan** (YOO·an), **Ifan** (II·vahn) and **Evan** (E·vahn).

Iola f. (YOH·lah) Feminine form of Iolo.

Iolo m. (YOH·loh) A common nickname for Iorwerth, often used as a name in its own right. Iolo Morganwg (Iolo of Glamorgan) was the bardic name of Edward Williams (1747–1826), stonemason, poet, scholar, and initiator of the modern National Eisteddfod.

Iorwerth m. (YOHR·wayrth) From Norse *iôr* 'lord' + Welsh *gwerth* 'value, worth'. From the Middle Ages to the present, Iorwerth has been used as a Welsh version of Edward.

Llinos f. (*LH*EE·nos) The Welsh word for 'linnet'.

Llio f. (*LH*EE·oh) Originally a nickname for Gwenllian. Llio is now a popular name in its own right.

Llwyd m. (*LH*OO·eed) From Welsh *llwyd* 'grey, holy'. The name is anglicized as **Lloyd.**

Llywelyn m. (*lh*u·WEL·een) From Welsh *llyw* 'leader, steerer' + *eilun* 'image'. Two princes who symbolize the greatest success and the bitterest failure of the medieval Welsh quest for independence were Llywelyn Fawr (Llywelyn the Great, 1173–1240) and Llywelyn yr Olaf (Llywelyn the Last, d. 1282). This is a popular patriotic name. Nicknames are **Llelo** (*LH*E·loh) and **Llew** (*LH*E·oo), which is also Welsh for 'lion'.

Lowri f. (LOW·ree) From Latin *laura* 'laurel'. This is a very popular name in North Wales.

Macsen, Maxen m. (MAK·sen) From Latin name Maximus. Maxen Wledig (Lord Maxen) was a 4th-century Spanish-born general who led the remnants of the Roman army out of Britain to claim to the emperorship. He was briefly successful.

Madoc m. (MAH·dog) From British *mad* 'fortunate, lucky'. According to legend, Madog ap Owain Gwynedd colonized North America in the late 12th century.

Maelgwn m. (MAYL·goon) From Welsh *mael* 'prince' + *ci (cwn)* 'wolf, hound'. Maelgwn Gwynedd was a 6th-century Welsh king.

Maelogan, Maelon m. (may·LOH·gahn, MAY·lon) From Welsh *mael* 'prince' + *-on,* a divine ending. A feminine version is **Maelona** (may·LOH·nah) 'divine princess', nicknamed **Lona** (LOH·nah).

Mair f. (MIIR) A Welsh form of Mary. Others are **Meira** (MAYR·ah) and **Mairwen** (MIIR·wen): Mair + *gwen* 'shining, holy'.

March m. (MAHR*X*) From Welsh *march* 'horse'. The name of King Mark in the Welsh version of the Tristan saga, in which he is known as March ap Meirchion (Horse, Son of Horses). The horse was a symbol of kingship in Celtic culture.

Marged f. (MAHR·ged) The Welsh form of Margaret. Variants are **Marared** (mahr·AHR·ed), **Mared** (MAHR·ed), and **Margiad** (MAHR·gyahd). A nickname is **Megan** (MEG·ahn).

Math m. (MAHTH) From Celtic **math* 'bear'. According to the *Mabinogi,* Math ap Mathonwy was king of North Wales and a powerful magician.

Meical m. (MAYK·al) The modern Welsh form of Michael. An older form is **Mihangel** (mi·HAHNG·el); a nickname is **Meic** (MAYK).

Melangell f. (mel·AHNG·*elh*) Melangell, the Welsh patron saint of animals, was a 6th-century Irish princess who hid a hare from the hounds, and was given land for a convent in Wales. In that area, the hare is called 'Melangell's little lamb', and until recently was not hunted.

Meleri f. (mel·AYR·ee) From Welsh *my* 'my' + Eleri, the name of a 5th-century saint, the grandmother of Saint David.

Meredith, Meredudd m. (me·RED·*ith*) From Welsh *mawr* 'great, big' + *udd* 'lord'. The name of many medieval princes. In America this has become a girls' name, but in Wales it is a boys' name.

Meriel, Meryl f. (MER·yel, MER·eel) Old Irish *muir* 'sea' + *gel* 'bright'.

Mona f. (MOH·nah) From Môn, the Welsh name for the island of Angelsey.

Morfudd, Morfydd f. (MOHR·vi*th*) Possibly from Welsh *mawr* 'great, big' + either *budd* 'benefit, victory' or *gwyd* 'sight, knowledge'. This was the name of a woman immortalized by the 14th-century poet Dafydd ap Gwilym. It is one of the most popular Welsh women's names.

Morgan, Morgant m. and f. (MOHR·gahn, MOHR·gahnt) From Welsh *môr* 'sea' or *mawr* 'great, big' + *can* 'bright' or *cant* 'circle' or *geni* 'born'. This name could mean anything from 'big circle' to 'sea-born'. The most famous Morgan is probably Morgan la Fée, King Arthur's half-sister and a famed sorceress.

Morwen f. (MOHR·wen) From Welsh *morwyn* 'maiden'. A variant is **Morwenna** (mohr·WEN·ah).

Myfanwy f. (muh·VAHN·wee) From Welsh *my* 'my' + *manwy* 'fine, rare'. Myfanwy is an archetypal Welsh woman's name, celebrated in a famous love poem, *Myfanwy Fychan* (1860) by John Ceiriog. Nicknames include **Myfi** (MUH·vee) and **Myfina** (muh·VEE·nah).

Myrddin m. (MUHR·*th*in) From British **moridunon* 'sea fortress'. The Welsh source of the name of the sorcerer Merlin. According to early legend, Myrddin was a warrior who went mad during the battle of Arderydd in 573, and lived for years in the forest of Celyddon, fearing death at the hands of his enemy, Rhydderch Hael, and composing poems of prophecy, philosophy and lament over his wretched state.

Nerys f. (NER·ees) From Welsh *nêr* 'lord', and a modern form of the medieval name Generys. Nerys is currently a very popular Welsh woman's name.

Nesta f. (NEST·ah) The most popular Welsh form of Agnes. Variants include **Annest** (AHN·nest) and **Nest** (NEST). The 11th-century Nest verch Rhys ap Tewdwr was known as 'Helen of Wales' for her beauty and the trouble it caused.

Nia f. (NEE·ah) The Welsh form of the Irish name Niamh, from the Old Irish *niam* 'luster, sheen, brilliance'.

Nona f. (NOH·nah) Nona was the mother of Saint David, the patron saint of Wales. She was also, it was said, a cousin of King Arthur. Nicknames are **Non** (NOHN) and **Nonita** (noh·NEE·tah). Saint Nona's feast day is March 2, the day after her son's.

Olwen f. (OHL·wen) From *ôl* 'track, trace' + *gwen* 'shining, holy'. In the early Welsh tale, *Kulhwch and Olwen,* Olwen was the daughter of a giant named Ysbaddaden.

Owein, Owain m. (OH·wayn) From Latin name Eugenius 'well-born'. Long a popular name.

Padrig m. (PAHD·rig) The Welsh form of Pádraig (Patrick), patron saint of Ireland, whose feast day is March 17.

Parry (PAHR·ee) m. From Welsh *ap Harri* 'son of Harry or Henry'. A very common name, though more often found as a middle or surname than a given name.

Pasgen m. (PAHS·gen) From Welsh Pasg 'Easter'.

Pawl m. (POWL) The Welsh form of Paul.

Pedr m. (PEDR) The Welsh form of Peter. Nicknames include **Pedran** (PED·rahn) and **Petran** (PET·rahn).

Pennar m. (PEN·ahr) From Welsh *pen* 'head' + *ardd* 'hill, height'.

Peredur m. (per·ED·eer) Of uncertain derivation, perhaps from Welsh *peri* 'spears' + *dûr* 'hard'. Peredur mab Efrawc was the hero of a Welsh Arthurian grail romance. A popular name.

Petra f. (PET·rah) The feminine form of Peter.

Pryderi m. (pra·DAYR·ee) In the *Mabinogi,* Pryderi was stolen by a monstrous claw on the night he was born and deposited in the stable of Teyrnon Twrf Fliant. Teyrnon named him Gwri Gwallt Euryn (Gwri Golden-Hair) and raised him, until it became clear that the boy was the missing son of Pwyll and Rhiannon. When Pryderi was returned to his mother, her first words were 'I would be relieved of my care (*pryder*) if this were true!' And so he was renamed Pryderi.

Prys m. (PREES) From *ap Rhys* 'son of Rhys'. Anglicized as Price.

Rhain m. (*RH*IIN) From Welsh *rhain* 'spear, lance'. A related name is **Rhainallt** (*RH*IIN-a*lht*): *rhain* + *allt* 'hill'.

Rhian f. (*RH*EE·an) From Welsh *rhiain* 'maiden'. **Rhiain** (*RH*EE·in) is also a name in its own right. Rhian is currently one of the more popular girls' names, possibly because it resembles the famous name Rhiannon.

Rhiannon f. (*rh*ee·AHN·on) From Celtic **Rigantona* 'divine queen'. According to legend, Rhiannon's birds sang more sweetly than any birds of the mortal world, but Rhiannon herself is notable for her habit of speaking her mind forthrightly and with wit.

Rhianwen f. (*rh*ee·AHN·wen) From Welsh *rhiain* 'maiden' + *gwen* 'shining, holy'.

Rhisiart m. (*RH*ISH·art) The Welsh form of Richard.

Rhodri m. (*RH*OD·ree) From Welsh *rhod* 'circle' + *rhi* 'ruler'. Rhodri Fawr (Rhodri the Great) was an important 9th-century king. He was a renowned warrior, as well as the ancestor of many of the later dynasties of Wales.

Rhonwen f. (*RH*ON·wen) Possibly from Welsh *rhon* 'spear' + *gwen* 'shining, holy'. A nickname is **Rhona** (*RH*OH·nah).

Rhydderch m. (*RH*UH*TH*·erx) From Welsh *rhi* 'king' + *derchafu* 'ascending'. Rhydderch Hael (Rhydderch the Generous) was a king of the Old North in the 6th century. He fought alongside Urien Rheged and Morcant against the incursions of Anglians into the area that is now southern Scotland.

Rhys m. (*RH*EES) From Welsh *rhys* 'ardor, passion'. A popular name throughout Welsh history, and a classic man's name. Anglicized as **Reece** or **Rice.**

Robat, Robet m. (ROB·at) The Welsh form of Robert. A nickname is **Robyn** (ROB·een). The 15th-century Robyn Ddu (Black Robin) and 19th-century Robyn Ddu Eryri (Black Robin of Snowdonia) were noted Welsh poets.

Selwyn m. (SEL·ween) From Welsh *sêl* 'ardour' + *gwyn* 'shining, holy'.

Seren m. and f. (SER·en) The Welsh word for 'star'. Sirona, from the same Celtic root, was an ancient Gaulish goddess of hot springs.

Siâm m. (SHAM) The Welsh form of James.

Siân f. (SHAN) A Welsh form of Jane. Nickname: **Siani** (SHAN·ee).

Siarl m. (SHARL) The Welsh form of Charles.

Siôn m. (SHON) A Welsh form of John. **Sioni** (SHON·ee) and **Sionyn** (SHON·een) are nicknames.

Sioned f. (SHON·ed) The Welsh equivalent of Janet.

Siôr m. (SHOR) The Welsh form of George.

Siwan f. (SHOO·ahn) The Welsh equivalent of Joan.

Sulien m. (SIL·yen) From Welsh *sul* 'sun' + *geni* 'born'. Originally the name of a Celtic sun god. An 11th-century Welsh bishop of Saint David's named Sulien was reputed to have been the most learned man in all of Wales.

Taliesin m. (tahl·YES·in) From Welsh *tâl* 'forehead, brow' + *iesin* 'radiant, shining'. A number of very early Celtic names contain the element *tal (dal)* 'forehead', perhaps a reflection of the Celtic obsession with heads and with wisdom. Taliesin was a Welsh poet of the 6th century who composed poems in praise of the heroes Owein, Urien Rheged and others. Though Taliesin was a real person, he entered Welsh mythology as the archetypal poet, a mystic who had been everywhere and seen everything since the dawn of time.

Tanwen f. (TAHN·wen) From Welsh *tân* 'fire' + *gwen* 'shining, holy'.

Tegan f. (TEG·ahn) From Welsh *teg* 'pretty, fine' + the diminutive *-an*. The name of an early saint and of a river in Ceredigion.

Tegau f. (TEG·ay) From Welsh *teg* 'fair, pretty, fine'. In legend, Tegau Eurfron (Golden-Breast) was the wife of Caradoc Freichfras (Strong-Arm) and one of the Three Faithful Women of the Island of Britain. She owned a mantle, one of the *Tri Thlws ar Ddeg Ynys Prydain* (The Thirteen Treasures of the Island of Britain), that would reach the ground only when worn by a chaste woman, and which become shorter the more faithless its wearer. Tegau was reputedly the only woman of King Arthur's court who could wear the mantle at full length.

Tegeirian f. (teg·AYR·yahn) From Welsh *teg* 'pretty, fine' + *eirian* 'beautiful'. Tegeirian is also the Welsh word for 'orchid'.

Tegwen f. (TEG·wen) *teg* 'pretty, fine' + *gwen* 'shining, holy'.

Teilo m. (TAY·loh) Teilo was a 6th-century saint who founded a church at Llandeilo Fawr in Dyfed. After his death, there arose a dispute among the churches of Llandeilo, Llandaf and Penally as to where Teilo's remains should be kept. The holy man's body miraculously triplicated, so that no one would be left out. Saint Teilo's feast day is February 9.

Teleri f. (tel·AYR·ee) From Welsh *ty* 'your' + Eleri, the name of an early saint and of a river in Dyfed. Teleri verch Peul was one of the maidens of King Arthur's court mentioned in the tale of *Kulhwch and Olwen.*

Teyrnon m. (TAYR·non) From Celtic *tigernonos* 'divine prince'. In the *Mabinogi,* Teyrnon Twrf Fliant (Teyrnon of the Tumult of the Sea) was Pryderi's foster father.

Tomos m. (TOHM·ohs) The Welsh version of Thomas. A nickname is **Twm** (TOOM). Twm Siôn Cati (1530–1609), an antiquarian, poet and outlaw, was known as the Welsh Robin Hood.

Trefor m. (TREV·ohr) From Welsh *tref* 'home, town' + *mor* 'great'. A name that has been used since the 10th century.

Tudur, Tudor, Tewdwr (TID·ir, TID·or, tee·OO·door) m. From Celtic *teutorigos* 'king of the tribe'. The name Teutates was mentioned by Roman writers as one of the gods of the Gaulish Celts. The word has an Indo-European origin, and in its Germanic form became *deutsch.* The name shows up regularly throughout Welsh history. Tewdwr ap Giffri was a 10th-century king of Brecon. Tudur Aled was a renowned Welsh poet of the (appropriately) early Tudor era.

Wmffre m. (OOM·free) The Welsh form of Humphrey.

BRITTANY

any of the Breton baby names suggested below were borne by Christian saints who lived as long ago as the 5th century. Their Celtic names can be found today in Brittany as the names of towns, villages, churches, cathedrals, islands, hills, wells and springs. City streets and country roads are graced by picturesque statues of the founding saints, and the worship of these revered holy people includes ritual processions and festivals on saints' feast days.

Brittany is a peninsula in the northwest of France, comprised of the departments of Finistère, Côtes-du-Nord, Ille-et-Vilaine and Morbihan. Continental Celts occupied the area before the days of the Roman Empire, but their culture and language were overwhelmed by a wave of immigration in the 5th and 6th centuries from across the Channel. Some of these immigrants from Britain were fleeing Anglo-Saxon armies, while others came as missionaries and settlers. These newcomers spoke British, a Celtic tongue that was also the precursor of Cornish and Welsh. Until the 9th century, these three languages were virtually identical, for even after the emigration of Britons to Brittany there was frequent communication across the Channel. During the Age of the Saints (450–600 AD), Celtic missionaries from Ireland and western Britain travelled back and forth often as they evangelized much of Europe, and it seems nearly every early Breton saint was born in Ireland, Wales or Cornwall.

Medieval Brittany was a duchy which, through strategic alliances with its neighbors, managed to remain fairly independent until the 15th century, when it became part of France. French had already become the language of the upper and learned classes in Brittany as early as 1200, and over the centuries, the area in which Breton was spoken receded to the far end of the peninsula—to Basse Bretagne, or Lower Brittany.

The only existing record of written Breton from before 1500, apart from notes in the margins of Latin manuscripts, are names of people and places found on official charters and deeds. Most of these early names are combinations Old Breton words such as *aour* 'gold', *argant* 'silver', *gwen* 'shining, holy', *mad* 'happy, lucky', and *lon* 'full'. From these early records, we know what many of the region's early inhabitants were called, but unless they were monarchs or saints, we know nothing more about them. Because men were more likely to own property than women, more men's names are known from that time.

Breton had the distinction of being the first Celtic language to appear in a printed book. Jehan Lagadeuc's *Catholicon,* published in 1499, was a French-Breton-Latin dictionary intended for priests who did not speak the language of their parishoners. From about 1500 AD onwards some Breton literature survives, though much early material was lost. We know that the French writers of tales of King Arthur used Breton oral tradition as their source, yet few related Breton manuscripts remain, and there is evidence that at least some early literature was deliberately destroyed. Fortunately, Breton storytellers preserved a rich and fascinating oral literature into the 20th century, and in the past century there has been a revival of Breton as a literary language.

About 250,000 people speak Breton today, though exact statistics are not available. The number is distributed unevenly, with nearly all Breton speakers in the oldest age groups. The language has received virtually no official recognition by French authorities, and has in the past been suppressed. Many Bretons remember a time when children were punished for speaking Breton in class, and when signs in public places read, *Il est interdit de cracher par terre et de parler Breton*—'It is forbidden to spit on the ground and to speak Breton'. All too often, parents in Brittany have been discouraged or even prevented from registering Breton names for their children. Attempts to reinstate the Breton language and names are closely tied to the separatist movement.

Giving a Breton name to a child today is often a political state-ment, and a decision about how to spell a Breton name is also political. By the early 20th century, local dialects differed so greatly that many Breton speakers couldn't communicate with one another. Attempts to bring the dialects closer together through a common spelling system have produced several ways of writing the language. *Zedacheg*, or 'unified spelling', was created during the Second World War with the sponsorship of the Vichy government. Although *Zedacheg* is the spelling system used by most writers and scholars, it is nevertheless tainted with bitter memories of Nazi occupation. The other major spelling system, 'university spelling', has the approval of the French government, a kiss of death in the eyes of Breton language activists. *Zedacheg* spelling is given for most of the names that follow, since most Breton name books use it. However, because most parents out-side Brittany will choose Breton names not for political reasons but for their sound, spelling and meaning, French spellings of Breton names are given when they seem more appealing, such as Annick for Annaig, and Corentin for Kaourantin.

Most Breton nicknames are formed by adding *-ig* to a name. However, in English an 'ig' sound is not particularly pleasing, and what's more, in Breton *ig* is pronounced 'eek'. For this reason, I have listed nicknames with their *-ic* or *-ick* spellings first, though purists consider them too French. You may change these to *-ig*, of course, if you wish. Breton nicknames are also formed by shortening a name, or by adding *-ou* (pronounced 'oo'). Feminine forms are created from men's names by adding *-a*, *-enn*, or *-ez* (pronounced 'ess'). For most of the following names, only the *-a* form is given, but an *-ez* or *-enn* endings are just as traditional.

Stress in Breton is on the next-to-last syllable, though it is not as strong as stress in English. Final syllables ending in *-n* are nasalized as in French, but the *n* is also pronounced. The vowel sound 'ay' is pro-nounced as a short sound, like a French *é* or Spanish *e*, not a drawn out American 'ay-ee'. The letter combination *c'h* is pronounced as in the Scottish 'loch' or German 'Bach'.

Alan m. (AH·lan) A traditional name among the Dukes of Brittany. Alan the Great defeated the Vikings at Questembert in 890. His grandson, Alan Barbetorte, drove the Vikings out of Brittany for good in 939. The Breton contingent of the forces of William the Conqueror introduced this name in England, where it became quite popular. The feast day of Saint Alan, a 6th-century bishop of Quimper, is November 27.

Alana f. (ah·LAH·nah) Feminine form of Alan.

Alar m. (AH·lahr) Alar is the name of the patron saint of goldsmiths and blacksmiths, and the protector of horses. His feast day is December 1. Nicknames include **Alaric** (ah·LAH·reek), **Laric** (LAH·reek).

Alor m. (AH·lohr) The name of a 6th-century bishop of Quimper who signed a peace treaty with the Roman Empire. Saint Alor is the patron saint of Trémeoc. His feast day is October 25.

Andrev (ahn·DRAY·oh) m. The Breton form of André. A nickname is **Drev** (DRAY·oh).

Andreva (ahn·DRAY·vah) f. Feminine form of Andrev.

Annick f. (AHN·eek) A Breton form of Ann. Saint Ann, the mother of the Virgin Mary, is the patron saint of Brittany. According to local legend, she was born there. Other Breton forms of the name are **Annaic** or **Annaig** (ah·NAH·eek).

Aouregan f. (ow·RAY·gahn) From Old Breton *aour* 'gold' + *gwenn* 'shining, holy'. A very popular woman's name in the Middle Ages, with twenty or so variations in spelling, including **Aouregon, Auruguen, Aureguen** and **Oregon.**

Arc'hantael, Argantael m. (ahr·XAHN·tel, ahr·GAHN·tel) From Old Breton *argant* 'silver, shining' + *hael* 'noble, generous'.

Argantlon f. (ahr·GAHNT·lohn) From the Old Breton *argant* 'silver, shining' + *lon* 'full'.

Argantlowen f. (ahr·gahnt·LOH·wen) From Old Breton *argant* 'silver, shining' + *lowen* 'joyful'.

Arzhel m. (AHR·zel) From the British *artos* 'bear' + *maglos* 'chief'. Saint Arzhel was born in Wales in 482, and founded a monastery in Brittany in the Forest of Broceliande. Famed as a magician, Arzhel was summoned to the court of King Childebert in Paris. After his death, Arzhel's name was invoked to end droughts. His feast day is August 16

Arzhela f. (ahr·ZAY·lah) Feminine form of Arzhel.

Arzhur, Arzhul m. (AHR·zoor, AHR·zool) From Celtic *artos* 'bear' or from the Latin name Artorius (also from an Indo-European bear word). In Breton tradition, the legendary King Arzhur (Arthur) was made a saint. His feast day is October 6. Several medieval Dukes of Brittany were named Arzhur.

Avenie f. (ah·VAY·nee) From the Celtic *aven, avon* 'river'. Variants include **Aven** (AH·ven)

Azenor f (ah·ZAY·nor) The Breton form of Elinor, a popular woman's name in Brittany since the Middle Ages. The traditional account of the 6th-century Saint Azenor's life seems to be a mixture of fairy tale and fantasy genealogy. As a young princess, Azenor took a vow of chastity, but was forced to marry Duke Hoël II. Because of false accusations by her stepmother, the young bride was locked in a tower. Later, the pregnant Azenor was thrown into the sea in a barrel. She floated to Ireland, giving birth along the way to Saint Budoc. Her feast day is December 7. Nicknames are **Noric, Norig** (NOH·reek).

Aziliz f. (ah·ZEE·leez) The Breton form of Cecilia and long a popular women's name in Brittany. Saint Cecilia is patron saint of music, and her feast day is November 22.

Berc'hed, Brec'hed f. (BAYR·*x*ed, BRAY·*x*ed) The Breton form of the name of the Irish saint, Brigid, whose feast day is February 1. A popular Breton name.

Bernez m. (BAYR·nes) The Breton form of Bernard.

Blaez, Bleiz m. (BLAYS) From the Old Breton word for 'wolf'.

Bleuzenn f. (BLOO·zen) The Middle Breton word for flower. Bleuzenn is probably cognate with the Welsh name, Blodwen, derived from *blodyn* 'flower' + *gwen* 'shining, holy'. The Breton Saint Bleuzenn has a feast day of November 24.

Brendan m. (BRAYN·dahn) After the 5th-century Irish Saint Brendan the Navigator, whose feast day is May 16. A popular name.

Brendana f. (brayn·DAH·nah) The feminine form of Brendan.

Brevalaer m. (bray·VAH·layr) From Old Breton *bran* 'raven' + *uualatr* 'prince'. This was the name of an early bishop, about whom little is known, except that his feast day is January 19.

Briac m. (BREE·ahk) The Breton form of the Irish name Brian. The 6th-century Breton Saint Briac has a feast day of December 22. A feminine form is **Briaca** or **Briaga** (bree·AHK·ah).

Briec m. (BREE·ayk) From the British name Brigacos, from Celtic **brig* 'high, mighty'. Born to a pagan family in Wales in the 5th century, Saint Brieg was converted by Saint Germain of Auxerre, France. Briec founded several monasteries in Brittany, including Saint-Brieuc. His feast day is May 1. Variant spellings include **Brieg, Brieuc** and **Brieug.**

Budoc m. (BOO·dok) From the Celtic **bud* 'victory'. The Irish-born Saint Budoc, son of Saint Azénor, founded a monastery on the island of Lavret, where he became a celebrated teacher. His feast day is December 8. Also spelled **Budog.**

Deniel, Denoel m. (DAY·nyel, day·NOH·el) Breton forms of Daniel. Deniel was the name of a founding saint of Brittany whose feast day is December 11.

Deniela, Denoela f. (day·NYEL·ah, day·noh·EL·ah) Feminine forms of Deniel, Denoel.

Derrien m. (DAY·ryen) An early Breton saint. After a pilgrimage to the Holy Land, Saint Derrien performed miracles and saved a nobleman's son, the future Saint Riok, from a dragon. His feast day is February 7.

Devi m. (DAY·vee) Breton form of David, the patron saint of Wales, who is revered in Brittany as well. His feast day is March 1.

Donan m. (DOH·nan) The name of a disciple of Saint Briec. His feast day is September 24. A variant spelling is **Tonan.**

Edern m. (AY·dern) From Welsh *edyrn* 'great'. Saint Edern was a Welsh hermit who went to Brittany in the 9th century. Edern welcomed to his hermitage a deer that was being chased by a hunter. Afterwards, it is said, the deer never left his side. The saint's feast day is August 26. A popular Breton name.

Ederna f. (ay·DAYR·nah) The feminine form of Edern.

Efflam m. (AY·flahm) Probably derived from the Celtic *flamm* 'flame'. According to legend, Efflam was a 6th-century Irish prince who took religious vows and travelled Brittany, where he defeated a dragon by invoking God's name and brought forth a sacred spring. His feast day is November 6. A popular Breton name.

Elara f. (ay·LAH·rah) The feminine form of Alar.

Elen f. (AY·len) The Breton form of Helen. Elen was the name of the sister of Konan Meriadeg, who led the Britons into Brittany in the 5th century. Nicknames for Elen include **Lena** (LAY·nah), **Lenaic** (lay·NAH·eek).

Enora f. (ay·NOH·rah) Saint Enora was the wife of Saint Efflam; both took vows of chastity after their marriage, yet remained together for the rest of their lives. Her feast day is October 14.

Erwan m. (AYR·wahn) Saint Erwan (1253–1303) is also known by the French name Yves. Erwan is patron saint of lawyers. As a church judge, he gained a lasting reputation because of his fairness and his special attention to the poor. His feast day is May 19. French variants of the name are **Ivo** (EE·voh) and **Yvon** (EE·vohn).

Erwana f. (ayr·WAH·na) Feminine form of Erwan. The variants **Ivona** and **Yvona** (both pronounced ee·VOH·nah) are popular.

Ewen, Even m. (AY·ven) Nothing is known of the life of Saint Ewen, though the name has been popular since earliest times. Ewen's feast day is May 3.

Frañsez, Fanch m. (FRAHN·ses, FAHNSH) The Breton forms of the French name François. Nicknames are **Soa** (SWAH) and **Soaic** (SWAH·eek).

Frañseza f. (frahn·SAY·zah) The Breton form of the French name Françoise. Nicknames are **Seza** (SAY·zah), **Sezaic** (say·ZAH·eek).

Gael m. (GA·el) A popular Breton name that may have originated as a nickname for Judikaël.

Gaela, Gaelle f. (ga·EL·a, GA·el) Feminine forms of Gael.

Girec, Gireg m. (GEE·rik) Saint Gireg was born in Wales in 547. In Brittany he founded a monastery near Lanmeur and a hermitage near Ploudaniel. His feast day is February 17. A popular name.

Gladez f. (GLAH·des) Similar to the Welsh name Gwladys (from Welsh *gwlad* 'land, nation, sovereignty'). The 7th-century Saint Gladez was the mother of Saint Kado. Her feast day is March 29.

Glen m. (GLAYN) From Old Breton *glenn* 'valley'. The name of an early Breton saint, whose feast day is September 11.

Govran m. (GOH·vrahn) An Old Breton word meaning 'smith'. This was the name of an 8th-century saint from Vannes whose feast day is November 16. Variants are **Gobrien** (goh·BREE·en) and **Gobrian** (goh·BREE·ahn).

Gralon (GRAH·lohn) m. From the Old Breton *grad* 'rank' + *lon* 'full'. Gralon was the name of a legendary king of Brittany, the hero of the legend of the doomed city of Ker-Is, which sank into the Bay of Douarnenez because of the wickedness of its people. Gralon escaped with the help of Saint Gwenole.

Gweltaz m. (GWAYL·tahs) There were probably several early Breton saints by this name, which is found in over fifty place names in Brittany. Currently a popular name.

Gwencalon m. and f. (gwayn·KAH·lohn) An old Breton name, from *gwenn* 'bright, shining' + *calon* 'heart'.

Gwenn f. (GWAYN) The Old Breton word meaning 'shining, holy'. Saint Gwenn Teirbron was the mother of four saints. Her feast day is October 18.

Gwennec, Gwenneg m. (GWAYN·ek) m. A diminutive of the Old Breton *gwenn* 'shining, holy'. Gwennec is the patron saint of Plouhinec. His feast day is November 6.

Gwenole m. (gway·NOH·lay) The name of a 6th-century saint who founded the monastery of Landévennec. His feast day is March 3.

Gwenvael m. (GWAYN·vel) An old Breton name, derived from *gwenn* 'shining, holy' + *mael* 'prince, chief'. The name of a saint about whom little is known. His feast day is December 23.

Helori m. and f. (hay·LOH·ree) An Old Breton name derived from *hael* 'generous'.

Heodez f. (hay·OH·days) A 6th-century Breton princess and saint. According to a legendary account of her life, she was decapitated by her brother Tangi on the basis of false rumors. She put her head back on, however, and was as good as new. Tangi then did penance and became a saint as well. Heodez died for real in 545. Her feast day is November 28.

Herve m. (HAYR·vay) Herve is the name of one of the most popular Breton saints, son of the bard Hyvarnion and his wife Rivanone. Herve was born blind, and was always accompanied by his guide Guiharan and his tame wolf. Traditionally he has been the patron saint of bards. His feast day is June 17. The Breton companions of William the Conqueror carried the name to England, where it became anglicized as Harvey.

Hoël m. (HOH·el) Hoël was a popular name among the Dukes of Brittany, and was also the name of the father of Morgan la Fay in several medieval French Arthurian tales.

Izold f. (EE·zohld) The Breton name for the heroine of the tale of Tristan and Isolde.

Jakez m. (ZHAH·kays) The Breton form of Jacques.

Jannet f. (ZHAH·nayt) The Breton form of Jeanne.

Jos m. (ZHOS) From the Old Bredon *iud* 'lord, chief'. A popular Breton name, originally a nickname for Judoc. This name was taken to England by Breton soldiers of William the Conqueror, and is the source of the English names Joyce and Jocelin.

Judikaël m. (zhoo·dee·KA·el) From the Old Breton *iud* 'lord, chief' + *hael* 'generous'. Judikaël was a 7th-century Breton king who left the throne for a life of monastic solitude. He has a feast day of December 16.

Kado, Kadec, Kadeg m. (KAH·doh, KAH·dek) From the Welsh *cad* 'battle'. The Breton form of the name of an early Welsh saint, Cadoc, who was also active in Brittany. His feast day is January 24.

Kanna f. (KAH·nah) An early saint whose feast day is March 10.

Kaourantin m. (kaoh·RAHN·teen) The name of a 5th-century saint who was bishop of Quimper. He is usually depicted holding a fish, the symbol of a miracle he was said to perform every day. He would place the bones of a fish he had eaten into a fountain, whereupon the bones would become a living fish again. His feast day is December 12. A popular Breton first name. A French spelling is **Corentin** (koh·REN·teen). Nicknames are **Tin** (TEEN), **Tinic, Tinig** (TEEN·eek), **Kaour** (KAOHR), and **Kao** (KAOH).

Katell, Katel f. (KAH·tel) The Breton form of Catherine. A nickname is **Katou** (KAH·too).

Kavan m. (KAH·vahn) From the Old Breton *kad* 'battle'. The name of an early saint whose feast day is March 10.

Klervi f. (KLAYR·vee) The name of a 6th-century saint, sister of Saint Gwenole. Her feast day is October 3. Also written **Clervie.**

Konan m. (KOHN·ahn) From Celtic **kuno* 'high, mighty'. In Breton legend, it was Konan Meriadeg who led fugitive Britons across the English Channel to Armorica, present-day Brittany. He is considered the ancestor of the Dukes of Brittany. A 7th-century Saint Konan has a feast day of September 28. Also written **Conan.**

Korneli m. (kohr·NAY·lee) Saint Korneli is venerated in the region of Carnac as the protector of horned beasts.

Koulm, Koulma f. (KOOLM, KOOL·mah) From Old Breton *koulm* 'dove'. A popular Breton name, borne by the daughter of Konan Meriadeg and by a Saint Koulma, whose feast day is December 25.

Kristen f. (KRIS·ten) The Breton form of Christine. Saint Kristen has a feast day of November 12. A variant is **Kristell** (KRIS·tel).

Lara f. (LAH·rah) The feminine form of Alar.

Leri, Lery m. (LE·ree) The name of a 7th-century hermit saint. His feast day is September 30.

Levenez f. (lay·VAY·nayz) The Breton word for 'happiness' and the name of an early saint whose feast day is November 3.

Loeiz m. (LOH·ayz) The Breton form of Louis.

Loeiza f. (loh·AY·zah) The feminine form of Loeiz.

Madenn f. (MAH·den) From Old Breton *mad* 'happy, lucky'. A popular name in the Middle Ages. Nicknames are **Madina** (ma·DEE·nah) and **Madezou** (mah·DE·zoo)

Malo m. (MAH·loh) From Old Breton *mach* 'hostage' + *lon* 'shining'. Malo was one of the most important early Breton saints, patron of St.-Malo. His feast day is November 15.

Marc'harit f. (mahr·*XAHR*·eed) The Breton form of Margaret, long a popular woman's name in Brittany.

Marrec m. (MAHR·ek) From an Old Breton word for horseman or knight.

Marzhin m. (MARH·zeen) The Breton form of Martin.

Mazhe m. (MAH·zay) The Breton form of Matthew.

Mazheva f. (mah·ZAY·vah) The feminine form of Mazhe.

Melan m. (MAY·lahn) A 5th-century saint and bishop of Rennes, whose feast day is January 6. Variant spellings include **Melen, Melaine** (both pronounced MAY·len).

Melle f. (MAY·lah) An Irish-born saint venerated in Brittany. The name is from the Old Irish word for lightning, *mall*. Saint Melle's feast day is March 9.

Menguy m. (MAYN·gee) Old Breton *men* 'stone' + *ki* 'hound, wolf'.

Meriadec, Meriadeg m. (may·REEAH·dek) Meriadeg was the name of a 7th-century saint and bishop of Vannes. His feast day is June 7. A variant spelling is **Meriadoc** (may·REEAH·dohk).

Meven m. (MAY·ven) The 6th-century Saint Meven founded the abbey of Saint-Méen in the Forest of Broceliande. The forest is real, but many fictional medieval romances were set there. On a trip to Rome, Meven reportedly dispatched a dragon that was bothering residents of the Loire valley. His feast day is June 21.

Mikael m. (MEE·kael, MEE·kel) The Breton form of Michel. A nickname is **Kaelic** (KAEL·eek, KEL·eek).

Mikaela f. (mee·KAEL·ah) Feminine form of Mikael.

Morgana, Morgane f. (mohr·GAH·nah) The Breton name for King Arthur's sister, Morgan la Fay, who was once considered a saint in

Brittany and given a feast day, October 8. Currently a popular Breton name. A variant is **Morganez** (mohr·GAH·nes).

Morvan m. (MOHR·vahn) From the Old Breton *mor* 'sea'. A name borne by a 9th-century Breton king.

Morvana f. (mohr·VAH·nah) Feminine form of Morvan. A nickname is **Vana** (VAH·nah).

Nedeleg m. and f. (nay·DE·lek) The Breton word for Christmas, the equivalent of the French or English name Noel.

Neven m. (NAY·ven) A popular Breton name, and the name of an early saint, whose feast day is April 6.

Nevena f. (nay·VE·nah) Feminine form of Neven.

Nikolaz m. (nee·KOH·lahs) The Breton form of Nicholas. Nicknames include **Kolaz** (KO·lahs), **Kolazic, Kolazig** (koh·LAH·zeek)

Nolwenn f. (NOHL·ven) From Welsh *noyal,* a place name + *gwenn* 'shining, holy'. Saint Nolwenn, daughter of a 6th-century prince of Cornwall, consecrated herself to God when young, and chose a life of solitude in the area around Vannes in Brittany. Her feast day is July 6. Currently a very popular name.

Nonn f. (NOHN) Saint Nonn was the mother of Saint David of Wales. She is especially venerated in Brittany, where many landmarks bear her name, including a hill, a chapel, an altar and a fountain. Her feast day is March 2. Nicknames include **Nonna** (NOH·nah) and **Nonnita** (noh·NEE·tah).

Oanez f. (WAH·nes) The Breton form of the name Agnes.

Olier m. (OH·lyay) The Breton form of the French name Olivier.

Padrig m. (PAH·dreek) The Breton form of the Irish name Pádraig (Patrick). Saint Patrick's feast day is March 17.

Padriga f. (pah·DREE·gah) The feminine form of Padrig.

Paol, Pol m. (PAOHL, POHL) Breton forms of Paul. The Breton Saint Pol Aurelian (492–572) was known as a slayer of dragons and a founder of monasteries, notably that of Saint-Pol-de-Léon. His feast day is March 12. A popular Breton name.

Paola, Pola f. (PAOH·lah, POH·lah) Feminine forms of Paol.

Per m. (PER) The Breton form of Pierre. A part-French part-Breton form of the name is **Pierrick.**

Riok m. (REE·ohk) From Old Breton *ri* 'king'. The name of an early Breton saint, disciple of Gwenole. His feast day is February 12. Variants are **Riec, Rieg** (REE·ek).

Rivanon f. (ree·WAH·nohn) The name may be cognate with the Welsh Rhiannon. In Brittany, Rivanon is revered as the mother of Saint Herve. Her feast day is June 19. This is a popular name, and is also spelled **Riwanon.**

Ronan m. (ROH·nahn) From an Old Irish name that means 'little seal'. Saint Ronan, a 6th-century Irish-born monk, founded a hermitage in the forest of Locronan in Brittany. His feast day is June 1. Currently a popular name in Brittany. A variant is **Reunan** (RUH·nahn).

Ronana f. (roh·NAH·nah) The feminine form of Ronan.

Roparzh m. (ROH·pers) The Breton form of Robert. Saint Roparz of Arbrissel (1045–1116) was named archbishop of Rennes, but he chose instead to live the life of a forest hermit. His feast day is February 24.

Rozenn f. (ROH·zen) The Breton word for 'rose', a popular woman's name in Brittany.

Samzun m. (SAHM·zoon) From the biblical name Samson. The 6th-century Saint Samson was born in Wales and led a footloose existence, establishing churches in Britain, Ireland and northern France. In Brittany, he founded the famous abbey of Dol. His feast day is July 28.

Seva f. (SAY·vah) A 6th-century saint, sister of Saint Tugdual. The parish of Sainte-Sève is dedicated to her. Her feast day is July 23.

Sterenn f. (STAY·ren) The Breton word for 'star'.

Sulgwen f. (SOOL·gwen) An Old Breton name, from *sul* 'sun' + *gwen* 'bright, shining'.

Tanet m. (TAH·net) An Old Breton name meaning 'afire'.

Tangi, Tanguy m. (TAHN·gee) m. From Old Breton *tan* 'fire' + *ki* 'hound, wolf'. The name of a 6th-century saint, the brother of

Saint Heodez. Saint Tanguy's feast day is November 27. This name has been used in Brittany at least since the 10th century, and has recently become quite popular.

Taran m. (TAH·ran) After a statue of an ancient Celtic thunder god with the name Taran inscribed on it was unearthed in Brittany in the 1700s, he was venerated as a saint. Taranis was the name of a deity worshipped by ancient Celtic people from Britain to Yugoslavia.

Treveur m. (TRAY·vuhr) The name of an early prince and saint, son of Saint Trifine. Treveur is the patron saint of Carhaix, Kergloff and Camlez. His feast day is November 8.

Trifin, Trifine f. (TREE·feen, tree·FEE·nah) Saint Trifine was the daughter of Wéroc, a 6th-century count of Vannes. According to legend, she married the tyrant Conomor and was put to death when she refused to turn over her land to him. She was then resuscitated by Saint Gweltas. Her feast day is July 21.

Tristan m. (TREE·stahn) A popular name in Brittany, from the name of the hero of the tale of Tristan and Isolde. A nickname is **Tanick** (TAH·neek).

Tristana f. (tree·STAH·nah) Feminine version of Tristan.

Tudi, Tudy m. (TOO·dee) A 6th-century saint who gave his name to Loctudy and l'Ile-Tudy. His feast day is May 9.

Tudual, Tugdual m. (TOO·dwahl) Probably from the same source as the Welsh name Tudur: Celtic *teutorigos* 'king of the land or tribe'. Saint Tudual was a 6th-century Welsh-born saint who founded several monasteries in Brittany. His feast day is November 30.

Yann m. (YAHN) Breton form of the French name Jean, the equivalent of the English name John. Nickname: **Yannick** or **Yannig** (YAH·neek). This is a classic Breton man's name.

CORNWALL

ornwall is a peninsula in southwest England. It is bounded on the north, west and south by the sea and on the east by the River Tamar, named for the Celtic river goddess Tamara. The name Cornwall derives from the old British *corn,* 'horn' and the Anglo-Saxon word for the Celts, *walas* or *wealas.* Thus, the Cornish are 'the Celts of the horn'. During the Bronze Age, Cornwall was known throughout Europe and the Mediterranean for its rich deposits of tin, a necessary ingredient for the making of bronze. It seems only fitting that a region that helped make warfare more deadly produced the literature of chivalry. King Arthur was said to have been born at Tintagel Castle on the Cornish coast, and the tales of Arthur and his knights began among the bards of Cornwall, Wales and Brittany.

The Cornish language derives from the British language. which was once spoken throughout the central and southern parts of the island of Britain. In the 5th century, Anglo-Saxons armies drove a wedge between Wales and Cornwall and sent a wave of southern British across the Channel to Brittany. From that time forward, speakers of the languages that would become Welsh, Cornish and Breton were physically separated, and although there was commerce between the three areas, the languages slowly diverged. The ease of sea travel between Cornwall and Brittany resulted in these languages being closer to each other than either is to Welsh (until the Middle Ages, it took six days to get from Cornwall to London by land, but only one day to sail from Cornwall to Brittany). Cornish and Breton first names are very similar in sound if not in spelling, and the names of the same early saints grace towns, churches, wells and other land-marks in both regions.

The Cornish language has left very few written records. Nearly all early writing in Cornwall was in either Latin, French (the language of the Norman conquest) or English. While some earlier works survive, nearly all literature in Cornish was written between 1575 and 1800. It is mostly religious, and includes Biblical dramas known as mystery plays. The most important early source of Cornish personal names is the Bodmin Manumissions, a list of slaves set free in Cornwall, which was written in the margins of a 10th-century copy of the Gospels.

Family names became established in Cornwall in the 14th and 15th centuries. Most of these family names were based on place names which in turn derived from saints' names, nearly all of which were old Cornish or Welsh personal names. At the same time that these Celtic family names were coming into existence, Celtic first names were being rapidly replaced by the same handful of European Christian names that were sweeping aside older names in England and the rest of Europe. By 1400, over half of all boy babies born in Cornwall were named either John, William, Robert, Richard or Ralph. Distinctively Cornish nicknames for these were formed by adding *-a* to English names, for example Willa for William and Hicca for Richard. Only the names of the most popular early saints survived as first names into the 18th and 19th centuries—Petrock, Piran, Colan and Costentyn. Names from other languages acquired distinctively Cornish forms over the years: Michael became Myghal, Jacob became Jago, and Christine became Chesten.

It is generally agreed that the Cornish language disappeared in 1777 with the passing of Dolly Pentraeth, the last monolingual speaker of Cornish, though the language continued to be spoken by bilingual individuals for some years afterwards. Cornish words, expressions and names have survived, however, as has a strong feeling of being a Celtic people with a unique heritage. Today there is an energetic revival of Cornish and of native names. The Gorsedh of the Bards, an association of poets and scholars interested in speaking and writing in Cornish, was founded in 1928. A person inducted into the

Gorsedh chooses a bardic name in the Cornish language. Besides the traditional personal names, Cornish words for flowers, trees, animals, and other natural objects are used as sources of bardic names, especially for women, since so few early Cornish women's names survive. This use of nature words as names is in keeping with Celtic tradition.

Most Cornish words can be pronounced as if they were British English words, except that the letter *s* is usually pronounced 'z'. Accent is nearly always on the next-to-last syllable. There are currently two systems for spelling Cornish, and spelling rules are hardly strict. Most names ending in *k* could as easily end in *c,* and *s* can be changed to *z*.

Ailla f. (Il·lah) From a Cornish word meaning 'most beautiful'.

Andras f. (AHN·dras) The Cornish form of the name of the ancient Celtic goddess of victory, Andraste. Andraste was invoked by Queen Boudicca of the British Iceni as she prepared to attack the Romans in 60 AD.

Arranz f. and m. (AHR·anz) The Cornish word for silver. Many early British and Continental Celtic names were formed from words for silver and gold.

Arthur m. (AHR·thuhr) From Celtic *artos* 'bear', or possibly from the medieval Latin name Artorius, which derives from the same Indo-European root. King Arthur was, according to tradition, born at Tintagel Castle on the coast of Cornwall.

Arthyen m. (AHRTH·yen) From the Celtic *artos* 'bear' + *gen* 'to bear', hence 'bear-borne'. The old British name Arctogenos is derived from the same root words.

Austell m. (AH·stel) A companion of Saint Samson, Austell founded a church in Cornwall. His feast day is June 28.

Banallen f. (bahn·AHL·en) From *banal,* the Cornish word for the flower of the broom plant. A woman's blonde hair is traditionally compared to the brilliant yellow of this flower.

Benesek m. (be·NEZ·ek) From the Latin name Benedictus. This name is found in the Bodmin Manumissions.

Berlewen f. (ber·LEW·en) The Cornish name for the planet Venus.

Bersaba f. (ber·SAH·bah) The Cornish form of the biblical name Bathsheba, popular until the 18th century.

Beryan f. (BER·yan) The patron saint of St. Buryan's. Her feast day is June 4.

Bideven m. (bi·DEV·en) From the Cornish word for 'hawk'.

Blyth m. (BLIITH) From the Cornish word for 'wolf'.

Branwalather m. (bran·wa·LATH·uhr) From Cornish *bran* 'raven' + *walather* 'leader'. A saint, the son of a Cornish king named Kenen. His feast day is February 9.

Breaca f. (BRAH·kah) From the Old Irish *brecc* 'freckled.' Saint Breaca traveled from Kildare in Ireland to Cornwall, where two churches are named for her. Her feast day is June 4.

Brengy m. (BREN·gee) From Cornish *bren* 'noble' + *gi* 'hound, wolf'. A name found in the Bodmin Manumissions.

Bryluen f. (bree·LOO·en) From the Cornish *breilu* 'a rose'.

Bryok, Breoc m. (bree·OHK) From the British name Brigacos, which is derived from the Celtic root **brig* 'high, mighty'. This was the name of a 5th-century Welsh saint who was also active in Cornwall and Brittany. His feast day is May 1.

Buthek, Bithek m. (BITH·ek) From the Celtic **bud* 'victory'. The name of a Breton saint venerated in Cornwall, whose feast day is December 8. The name is a masculine equivalent of the name of Queen Boudicca of the Iceni, who led a rebellion against the Romans in 60 AD.

Cadan m. (KAHD·an) From British *cad* 'battle'.

Cador m. (KAHD·ohr) From British *cad* 'battle' + *wur* 'man'. Cador was a legendary ruler of Cornwall in the Dark Ages.

Carantoc m. (ka·RAN·tahk) From Cornish *carant* 'love'. The name of an early saint who was venerated in Cornwall, Brittany and Wales. His feast day is May 16.

Carrow m. (CAR·aw) From Celtic **cornu-* 'horned'. The Cornish word for 'deer'.

Casvelyn m. (kaz·VEL·uhn) From British *cad* 'battle' + Belinos, the name of a Celtic fire god. This is the Cornish form of the name Cassivellaunos, the father of the British King Caractacus.

Caswyn m. (KAZ·win) From Cornish *cad* 'battle' + *gwen* 'shining, holy'.

Chesten f. (CHEST·en) A Cornish form of the name Christine. This was a popular name in the 17th century.

Clesek m. (KLEZ·ek) From British **kluto* 'fame, renown'.

Colan, Collen m. (KOHL·uhn) From Welsh *collen* 'hazel tree'. The name of a 7th-century Welsh saint who slew a fierce giantess that was infesting the Vale of Llangollen. Colan also wrestled a pagan giant named Bras to see whose religion would prevail in Britain. Colan won. His feast day is May 21. This was a popular Cornish name up until the 18th century.

Columba f. (koh·LUM·ba) The Latin word for 'dove'. Columba was an early Cornish saint. Her feast day is November 13.

Conan m. (KAH·nan) From Celtic **kuno* 'great, high'. The name of a legendary Cornish king as well as a real 18th-century bishop of Cornwall. Another form of the name is **Kenan** (KEN·an).

Conwenna f. (kawn·WEN·ah) From Cornish *ci (cun)* 'wolf, hound' + *gwen* 'shining, holy'. According to the fictional history of Britain by Geoffrey of Monmouth, Conwenna was the mother of Belinus and Brennius, two early kings of Cornwall.

Cordelia f. (kohr·DEEL·yah) A traditional Cornish name, and the name of the faithful daughter in Shakespeare's *King Lear*. An early form was **Cordula** (kohr·DOO·lah).

Corentyn m. (koh·REN·tin) The name of a Cornish-born saint who became the first bishop of Quimper in Brittany. His feast day is May 1.

Costentyn m. (kahs·TEN·tin) The Cornish form of Constantine. Saint Costentyn was a Cornish king who gave up his throne to become a monk. His feast day is March 9. This was a popular name until the 18th century.

Cryda, Creeda f. (KREE·dah) From the Old Irish name, Créd. Saint Creed was an Irish princess who took religious vows, traveled, and founded several churches in Cornwall and Ireland. Her feast day is November 30.

Cuilliok m. (KWIL·yok) The Cornish word for 'soothsayer'.

Daveth m. (DAH·veth) The Cornish form of David, patron saint of Wales. His feast day is March 1.

Delen, Dellen f. (DEL·en) From the Cornish word for 'petal'. The diminutive form is **Delennyk** (del·EN·uhk).

Denzel, Denzil m. (DEN·zel) A place name that became a first name.

Derowen f. (der·OH·wen) From Celtic *derw* 'oak'.

Derwa f. (DER·wah) From Celtic *derw* 'oak'. The name of an early Cornish saint.

Donyerth, Donyarth m. (DON·yerth) The Cornish form of the old British name Dubnogartos, probably meaning 'black ridge'.

Dywana f. (de·WAH·nah) A legendary Cornish queen.

Elestren f. (el·ES·tren) From *laister*, the Cornish word for the flower 'iris'.

Elowen f. and m. (el·OH·wan) From *elew*, the Cornish word for 'elm'.

Endelyon f. (en·DEL·yon) The name of an early Cornish saint. Her feast day is April 29.

Esyld f. (ez·EELD) From the British *adsiltia* 'she who is gazed at'. The heroine of the tale of Tristan and Isolde, which was set in Cornwall. Esyld was a common woman's name in the Middle Ages. A variant is **Issot** (i·SOT).

Gawen m. (GOW·en) The Cornish form of the name Gawain. This was the name of King Arthur's nephew, the boldest of his knights. Gawen remained a popular Cornish man's name through the late 17th century.

Gelvinak m. (gel·VIN·ak) The Cornish name for the bird 'curlew', and the bardic name of Richard Gendall, editor and activist for Cornish language revival.

Gerens m. (GER·enz) From the Celtic *gerontios* 'old'. This is the later Cornish form of the name Geraint, hero of Arthurian romance and a legendary king of Cornwall. A consistently popular name.

Glastenen m. (glahs·TEN·en) From the Cornish word for 'scarlet oak'.

Glewas, Glewyas m. (GLOO·ahs, GLOO·yahs) From the Cornish *glew* 'clear, bright'. The name of an early saint, nephew of Saint Petroc. His feast day is May 3.

Golvan m. (GOHL·van) The Cornish word for 'sparrow', which was used as the bardic name of N.J.A. Williams, a Cornish scholar, poet, and playwright.

Gorlas m. (GOHR·laz) Cornish for 'very pure'. The name of the first husband of Ygerna, mother of King Arthur. Gorlas was Duke of Cornwall.

Gorneves m.(gohr·NEV·ez) From the British *vornemetos* 'very holy'. An old Cornish name.

Goron m. (GOHR·ohn) Cornish for 'hero', and the name of an early saint associated with a sacred cave and well near Gorron. His feast day is April 7.

Gorthelyk m. (gohr·THEL·ik) Cornish for 'very beloved'. A name found in the Bodmin Manumissions.

Gourgy m. (GOOR·gee) From British *gur* 'man' + *ci (cun)* 'hound, wolf'. A name found in the Bodmin Manumissions.

Gwenifer f. (GWEN·i·fer) The Cornish form of the Welsh name, Gwenhwyfar (Guenivere). See also Jenifer.

Gwennol f. (GWEN·ohl) The Cornish name of the bird 'swallow'.

Gwynek m. (GWIN·ek) Cornish for 'little fair one'. The name of an 8th-century saint associated with the parish of Saint Winnoc.

Hicca m. (HIK·uh) A Cornish nickname for Richard.

Jacca m. (JAHK·uh) The Cornish form of Jack.

Jago m. (JAHG·oh) The Cornish form of Jacob.

Jammes, Jamma m. (JAM·uhs, JAM·uh) The Cornish forms of James.

Jenifer f. (JEN·i·fer) The Cornish form of Welsh name Gwenhwyfar (Guenivere). The spelling with one *n* is traditional.

Jenifry f. (JEN·i·free) Probably the Cornish form of the Welsh name Gwenfrewi. Saint Gwenfrewi was an early marytr saint whose feast day is November 3.

Jenna, Jana f. (JEN·uh, JAN·uh) Early Cornish forms of Jane, from the Norman French Jonet. Another form is **Jowna** (JOWN·uh or JOHN·uh).

Jory m. (JOH·ree) A Cornish nickname for George.

Jowan m. (JOO·an, JOH·an) The Cornish form of John.

Jowanet f. (JOO·a·net) The Cornish feminine form of John.

Kayna, Keyne f. (KAYN·ah, KAYN) From Welsh *cain* 'beautiful'. The name of a 6th-century saint, born in Wales, patron of St. Keyne in Cornwall, the site of her holy well. Kayna refused all suitors, choosing instead a life of religious solitude. According to folk tradition, the first one of a married couple to drink from her well will dominate the relationship.

Kea m. (KAY) Probably from the Latin name Caius. The name of a 6th-century Cornish saint, and also of King Arthur's right-hand man. The two figures seem to be aspects of one real or legendary person, since, according to an early biography, Saint Kea went to see Guenivere after King Arthur's death and persuaded her to become a nun. The saint has a feast day of November 5.

Kelyn f. (KEL·uhn) The Cornish word for 'holly'.

Kensa f. (KEN·zah) From a Cornish word meaning 'first'.

Kerenza, Kerensa f. (ke·REN·zah) Cornish for 'love, affection'.

Keresyk, Kerezik m. (ke·REZ·ik) From British *caractacus* 'amiable', which was also the name of a king of early Britain. A variant spelling is **Carasek** (ka·RAZ·ek).

Kerra f. (KER·ah) The Cornish word for 'dearest'.

Kevern m. (KEV·ern) A 6th-century Cornish saint. His feast day is November 18.

Kitto m. (KIT·oh) A Cornish nickname for Christopher.

Lowenek f. (loh·EN·ek) From Cornish *lawenes* 'happiness, joy'.

Mabyn f. (MAB·uhn) From the British *mab* 'son, boy'. The name of a 6th-century Cornish saint whose feast day is September 21.

Madron, Madern m. (MAD·ruhn, MAD·uhrn) From British *mad* 'lucky, fortunate'. This was the name of an early Cornish saint whose well was the source of miraculous cures until the 1800s. His feast day is May 17.

Manacca f. (ma·NAH·kah) An early Cornish saint and abbess, sister of Saint Seleven. Her feast day is October 14.

Margh m. (MAHR) The Cornish word for 'horse', and the name of the King of Cornwall in the tale of Tristan and Isolde.

Mariot f. (mah·REE·ot) A Cornish nickname for Mary.

Marrek m. (MAHR·ek) Cornish for 'horseman'.

Marya f. (mah·REE·ah) The Cornish form of Mary.

Masek m. (MAHZ·ek) The Cornish form of the Welsh name, Madog, which means 'lucky, fortunate'.

Mawgan m. (MAW·gan) From British *maglo* 'prince' + *ci (cun)* 'hound, wolf'. The name of a 6th-century Cornish saint, whose feast day is September 26. Mawgan was a popular name in 17th-century Cornwall.

Melwyn f. (MEL·win) From the Cornish *mel* 'honey' + *gwyn* 'shining, holy'.

Melyonen f. (mel·YOHN·en) From the Cornish word for the flower, 'violet'.

Melyor, Meliora f. (MEL·yohr, mel·YOHR·ah) From the Cornish *mel* 'honey'. A very old Cornish name that was popular in the 17th and 18th centuries.

Meryasek m. (mer·YAZ·ek) The name of an important early Breton saint, also known as **Meriadek** or **Meriadoc,** who was the subject of a medieval drama *Bewnans Meryasek,* one of the few remaining pieces of early literature in the Cornish language. His feast day is June 7.

Meryn, Merryn m. (MER·uhn) An old Cornish name. Saint Meryn's feast day is January 6.

Milyan m. (MIL·yahn) Probably from Latin *aemilianus* 'flattering'. A name found in the Bodmin Manumissions. Also the name of a legendary king of Cornwall and an early saint whose feast day is November 6.

Morgelyn f. (mohr·GEL·in) The Cornish word for 'sea holly'.

Morvoren f. (mohr·VOHR·en) The Cornish word for 'mermaid'.

Morwenna f. (mohr·WEN·ah) From Cornish *mor* 'sea' + *gwen* 'bright, shining'. Saint Morwenna's feast day is July 5.

Morwennol f. (mohr·WEN·ol) From Cornish *mor* 'sea' + *gwennol* 'sparrow'. The bardic name of Phoebe Proctor, a Cornish writer.

Myghal m. (muh·HAYL) The Cornish form of Michael.

Nadelek m. (nah·DEL·ek) The Cornish word for Christmas.

Nessa f. (NES·ah) Cornish for 'second'.

Newlyna f. (noo·LEE·nah) The name of an early saint. Her feast day is April 27.

Neythen m. (NII·then) The name of a Cornish saint, who, according to legend, was beheaded by a group of robbers he was trying to convert. Neythen then picked up his head and walked the half mile back to his hut. His feast day is June 17.

Nicca m. (NIK·uh) A Cornish nickname for Nicholas.

Nonna f. (NAW·nuh) Patron saint of Altarnon and Pelynt. Nonna is especially venerated in Wales and Brittany as the mother of Saint David, patron saint of Wales. Her feast day is March 2.

Padern m. (PAH·dern) From the Latin *paternus* 'father'. The name of an early Cornish chieftain.

Pasco, Pascow (PAS·kaw) m. From Cornish *Pask* 'Easter'. A popular name until the mid-18th century.

Pawly m. (PAWL·ee) The Cornish form of Paul.

Peder m. (PAYD·er) The Cornish form of Pater.

Pencast m. (PEN·cast) The Cornish word for Pentecost. A popular name until the late 19th century.

Petrock, Pedrog, Pedrek m. (PET·rok, PED·rok) Saint Petrock and Saint Piran were the two most important saints of early Cornwall. Saint Pedrog founded a monastery at Padstow in the 6th century. He is usually depicted with a stag, based on a legend in which he protects the animal from hunters. His feast day is June 4.

Piran, Pirran, Peran, Perran m. (PEER·an, PER·an) Saint Piran was an Irish monk (probably named Ciarán in Irish) who traveled to Cornwall and founded a monastery. His feast day, March 5, is celebrated as the Cornish National Day. The Cornish flag bears the cross of St. Piran. This was a popular man's name through the 19th century.

Rewan, Rumon m. (ROO·an, ROO·man) An early Cornish bishop and saint whose feast day is August 30. This name is also found in the Bodmin Manumissions.

Rozen f. (ROH·zen) f. The Cornish word for 'rose'.

Rozenwyn f. (roh·ZEN·win) Cornish for 'shining rose': *rozen* + *gwyn* 'bright, shining'.

Ryol m. (REE·ol) From British *rigalis* 'king'. The name of the king in the Cornish drama *Bewnans Meryasek*. Also found in the Bodmin Manumissions as a personal name.

Seleven m. (ze·LEV·en) An early Cornish saint whose feast day is October 14.

Senara f. (ze·NAH·rah) An early saint, patron of Zennor.

Sevi f. (ZEV·ee) The Cornish word for 'strawberry'.

Silyen m. (SIL·yen) From British *sul* 'sun' + *genos* 'born'. The patron saint of Laxulyan. His feast day is July 29.

Sithny m. (SITH·nee) From Celtic **sith* 'peace'. Sithny is the patron saint of mad dogs. According to tradition, God revealed to him that he was going to be the patron saint of girls. The saint was unhappy with this, so God threatened to make him the patron saint of mad dogs instead. Saint Sithney replied, 'I'd rather have mad dogs than women any day!' His feast day is August 4, when sick dogs are taken to drink at his well.

Talan m. (TAHL·an) From Cornish *tal* 'forehead'. A name found in the Bodmin Manumissions.

Talek m. (TAHL·ek) From Cornish *tal* 'forehead'. The bardic name of E.G.R. Hooper, third Grand Bard of the Cornish Gorsedh.

Talwyn f. (TAHL·win) From *tal* 'forehead' + *gwyn* 'bright, shining'.

Tamara f. (tah·MAHR·ah) The name of the goddess of the river Tamar, the traditional boundary between England and Cornwall.

Tamon f. (TAM·on) From the Cornish word for the plant 'sea-pink'. The bardic name of Mary Truran, youngest person to become a member of the Cornish Gorsedh of the Bards.

Tamsyn f. (TAM·zuhn) The medieval Cornish feminine diminutive of Thomas. The name was popular up to the 18th century and then fell out of use, but it is making a comeback.

Teca f. (TEK·ah) The Cornish word for 'fairer'.

Tressa f. (TRES·ah) The Cornish word for 'third'.

Trevedic m. (tre·VED·ik) From a Cornish word meaning 'country dweller'.

Tristan, Trystan m. (TRIST·ahn) From the British name Drustan. In Arthurian Romance, the name of the nephew of King Margh (Mark) of Cornwall, and lover of Esyld (Isolde).

Uther m. (OOTH·er) The name of King Arthur's father, Uther Pendragon. Uther was popular as a Cornish man's name in the 16th and 17th centuries.

Wilmot, Wylmet f. (WIL·met) A Cornish feminine form of William. It fell out of use after the 18th century, but has made a comeback.

Wella m. (WEL·ah) A Cornish nickname for William.

Withell m. (WITH·el) A Cornish word for 'lion'.

Wyllow m. (WIL·oh) The name of a 6th-century saint. The church of Lanteglas is dedicated to him.

Ygerna, Igerna f. (ig·AYR·nah) Cognate with Welsh *eigr* 'fair maiden'. The name of King Arthur's mother, who was the wife of Gorlas, Duke of Cornwall.

Zethar m. and f. (ZETH·ahr) The Cornish word for 'seagull'.

ISLE OF MAN

The Isle of Man is located in the Irish Sea, just thirty miles from the coasts of Ireland and Wales and sixteen miles from Scotland. On a clear day, the island can be seen from the shores of all three. *Manu* was the earliest name for the island in the Old Irish language. Today it is known in Manx as either *Mannin* or *Ellan Vannin* (*ellan* 'isle' + the genitive case of *Mannin*). Some claim that the isle got its name from the Celtic sea god, Mananann, son of Lir, but the Manx people say that Mananann took his name from the island, which was reputedly his home in the mythic past.

The earliest writing on Man is carved on stone memorial markers dating from around 200–400 AD, and consists of Latin, British, Old Irish and Norse personal names in ogam, a writing system of straight and diagonal lines, a sort of code that was based on the letters of the Latin alphabet. The Celtic names that appear on these monuments include Ambecatos (Great Warrior), Drui (Druid), Kunovalos (High and Mighty) and Cu Magli (Hound of a Chief; hound was a flattering name for a man in the Celtic languages). The variety of names found inscribed on these stones reveals that Man was a busy way-station for traders and travelers of many lands.

During the Age of Saints, from 450–600 AD, Irish culture came to dominate the island, and churches and other landmarks throughout Man bear the names of Irish saints such as Patrick, Brigid and Colm Cille. In the 8th century, Man was conquered by the Vikings and though it remained under Norse rule for four hundred years, the Irish language remained dominant until 1266, when the island was annexed by Scottish kings. It passed into the ownership of English landlords in around 1400, and in 1765 became part of England. The island is now a self-governing community under the British Crown.

Throughout the Middle Ages the principal language spoken on the Isle of Man was virtually identical to Irish and Scottish Gaelic, even though Norse-speaking Vikings held power. After the island came under British rule, the Manx language survived official attempts to replace it entirely with English, and continued to be spoken well into the 20th century. The last fluent Manx speaker died in 1974. The language continues to be taught in schools, and its use is encouraged by organizations such as *Yn Çheshaght Ghailckagh,* the Manx Language Society, which was formed in 1899, and which has as its motto *Gyn chengay, gyn cheer*—'Without tongue, without country'.

In 1610, *The Anglican Book of Common Prayer* was translated into Manx, marking the language's first appearance in a printed book. From that date until the late 19th century, when local history, legends, folktales and folksongs were collected and published, only religious texts were available in Manx. The spelling of the language is strongly influenced by English, and is less able to convey the nuances of Celtic pronunciation than are the Irish and Scottish Gaelic spelling systems.

Today, many of the old Manx personal names are still used on the island. Some derive from Old Irish names, while others are Manx versions of names from languages of present and previous dominant cultures: English, Norse and Norman French. The Manx language developed its own forms of the common European Christian names, such as Juan for John and Moirrey for Mary. Unique to the Isle of Man are women's names based on the Old Irish word *cailleac* meaning 'nun, female devotee'—Calypatric and Calycrist, for example. These are feminine counterparts to Manx, Irish and Scottish men's names such as Gilpatrick 'servant of Saint Patrick' or Gilmartin 'servant of Saint Martin'.

Affrica f. (AW·free·kuh) The derivation of this name is uncertain, but it is probably not related to the name of the continent. This was a popular woman's name in the Middle Ages. The most famous Affrica, daughter of Godred, King of Man, founded a monastery in County Down in Ireland. Also written **Aufrica.**

Aimil f. (AY·mil) The Manx form of Emily.

Aleyn m. (AL·uhn) Probably from the Old Irish name Ailín, derived from *ail* 'noble'.

Alister m. (AWL·uhs·tuhr) The Manx form of Alexander, introduced by way of Scotland, where Alistair has long been a favorite name. Another Manx form is **Alistryn** (AWL·is·truhn).

Alistryna f. (awl·is·TREE·nuh) Feminine form of Alister and Alistryn.

Andreays m. (ahn·DRAY·uhs) The Manx form of the Greek name Andreas.

Anghus m. (AHN·guhs) From the Old Irish *oen* 'one' + *gus* 'vigor'. The Manx equivalent of the popular Scottish and Irish name.

Ascon m. (AS·kohn) From the name of an early Irish saint active on Man, Easconn.

Austeyn m. (AWS·ten) The Manx form of Augustine.

Bahee, Bahy f. (BAH·ee) Perhaps derived from the Old Irish *betha* 'life'. A longtime favorite woman's name on Man.

Blaanid f. (BLAH·nid) From the Old Irish name Bláthnat: *bláth* 'flower' + *-nat,* a diminutive. In legend, the name of a Manx princess, and also of Saint Brigid's cook.

Bradan, Braddan m. (BRAH·duhn) From the name of a Cornish saint. The parish of Kirk Braddan on Man is dedicated to him.

Bree f. (BREE) From the Old Irish name Bríd (Brigid), derived from the Celtic *brig* 'high, noble'. The parish of Kirk Bride on Man is dedicated to her.

Brian m. (BREE·uhn) The derivation of the name is not certain, but may be from the Celtic root *brig* 'high, noble'. A consistently popular name on Man since early times.

Callan m. (KAH·luhn) From the Old Irish name Ceallachán, The derivation of this name is not certain; it may mean 'someone who frequents churches' or 'someone who is warlike'.

Calybrid f. (KAH·lee·breed) From the Old Irish *cailleac* 'nun, woman devotee' + Bríd 'of Saint Brigid'.

Calycrist f. (KAH·lee·kreest) 'Woman devotee of Christ'.

Calypatric f. (kah·lee·PAHR·eek) 'Woman devotee of Saint Patrick'.

Calyvorra f. (kah·lee·VOH·ruh) 'Woman devotee of Mary'.

Cane m. (KAYN) from the Old Irish name Cathán: *cath* 'battle' + the diminutive *-án*.

Carbry m. (KAHR·bree) From the Old Irish name Cairbre. The parish of Kirk Arbory on Man is dedicated to an Irish saint by this name, whose feast day is May 3.

Catreena f. (kah·TREE·nuh) The Manx form of Catherine.

Colum m. (KAW·luhm) From the name of the Irish saint, Colum Cille, whose name derives from Latin *columba* 'a dove' + Old Irish *cille* 'church'.

Conan m. (KOH·nuhn) From Celtic **kuno* 'great, high'. Saint Conan of Man was the first Bishop of Sodor in the 7th century. His feast day is January 26.

Conchor m. (KAWN·uhr) From the Old Irish name Conchobar: *cú (con)* 'hound, wolf' + *cobar* 'desiring'.

Connaghyn m. (KAWN·a·huhn) From the Old Irish *cú (con)* 'hound, wolf' + *cenn* 'head'. The name of an early saint, possibly born on Man, commemorated in the parish of Onchan.

Corcan m. (KAWR·kuhn) From the Old Irish *corc* 'heart' + *-án*, the diminutive suffix.

Cowan m. (KOW·uhn) From the Old Irish name Comgán. This was the name of an 8th-century saint who founded churches in both Ireland and Scotland; he may have been active in Man as well. Comgán's feast day is October 13

Cowel m. (KOW·uhl) From the Old Irish name, Comgall. The 6th-century Irish Saint Comgall was the teacher of many great Irish missionary saints. His feast day is May 10.

Cristall m. (KRIS·tuhl) A Manx form of Christopher.

Donal m. (DAWN·uhl) From the Old Irish name Domnall: *domun* 'world' + *gal* 'ardor, valor'. Several Manx chieftains and saints have borne this name. Nicknames: **Dolen, Dolyn** (DAW·luhn).

Doncan m. (DAWNG·kuhn) From the Old Irish Donnchad: *donn* 'brown' or 'chief' + *cath* 'warrior'.

Doolish m. (DOO·lish) The Manx form of Douglas, from the Old Irish *dub* 'dark, black' + *glas* 'green or blue'.

Dorrin f. (DOHR·in) From the Old Irish name Doireand, possibly meaning 'daughter of Finn'.

Dugal m. (DOO·guhl) From the Old Irish name Dubgall: *dubh* 'dark' + *gall* 'a stranger'. The name of a prince of Man.

Ealisaid f. (el·uhs·AYD) The Manx form of Elizabeth.

Ealish f. (EE·lish) The Manx form of Alice.

Eoin m. (YOH·een) A Manx form of John. Two early bishops of Man bore this name.

Fenella f. (fe·NE·luh) From the Old Irish name Fionnuala: *finn* 'fair, bright' + *gúala* 'shoulders'. The name of an early queen of the Isle of Man.

Ferghus m. (FER·uhs) From the Old Irish name Fergus: *fer* 'man' + *gus* 'strength, vigor'.

Finlo m. (FIN·loh) From the Old Irish name Finnlug: *finn* 'bright, shining' + Lugh, the name of a Celtic god.

Finn, Fynn (FIN) m. An Old Irish name meaning 'bright, shining'.

Garmon m. (GAHR·muhn) From Latin name Germanus 'a German'. Garmon was a saint of the early 5th century, probably born in Brittany, but active in Wales, Ireland and the Isle of Man, where he served as bishop. His feast day is July 3. Sometimes found as **Jarmon, Jarman** (JAHR·muhn).

Gilandrew m. (gil·AHN·droo) From Old Irish *gilla* 'servant, devotee' + Andrew 'of Saint Andrew'.

Gilbrid m. (gil·BREED) 'Servant of Saint Brigid'.

Gilchrist m. (gil·KREEST) 'Servant of Christ'.

Gilcolm m. (gil·KAWLM) 'Servant of Saint Columba'.

Gilmartyn m. (gil·MARH·tuhn) 'Servant of Saint Martin'.

Gilmore m. (gil·MOHR) 'Servant of Mary'.

Gilno m. (GIL·noh) 'Servant of the saints'.

Hugh m. (HYOO) A name widely used as an English version of the Manx name Aedh. Nicknames: **Huchon** (HUH·chuhn), **Hugen** (HUH·guhn).

Ibot f. (I·buht) A nickname for Ysbal.

Illiam m. (IL·yuhm) A Manx form of William, and the name of two bishops of Man.

Jamys m. (JAY·muhs) The Manx form of James.

Johnet f. (JOH·nuht) The Manx form of Janet.

Jonee, Jony f. (JOH·nee) The Manx feminine forms of John.

Juan m. (JOO·uhn) The Manx nickname for John.

Kerron m. (KER·uhn) Manx version of the Old Irish name Ciarán: *ciar* 'black' + the diminutive *-án*.

Laurys m. (LEOO·ruhs) The Manx form of Lawrence.

Loghlin m. (LAW*X*·luhn) From the Old Irish Lochlainn, a name for the homeland of the Vikings.

Lonan m. (LAWN·uhn) From the Old Irish *lon* 'blackbird' + the diminutive *-án*. A 6th-century Irish Saint Lonan was noted for the size of his library.

Lugh m. (LOO) From the Celtic **lugu* 'bright'. The name of a Celtic god, found in both Irish and Welsh mythology. It is also recorded as a personal name on Man.

Machonna m. (mah·*X*AW·nuh) From the Old Irish *ma* 'my' + *cú (con)* 'hound, wolf'. The 6th-century Manx Saint Machonna has a feast day of November 12.

Malew m. (mah·LOO) From Old Irish *ma* 'my' + the god-name Lugh, from Celtic **lugu* 'bright'. Malew was an early Manx saint; Kirk Malew (Malew Church) is dedicated to him.

Manus m. (MAH·nuhs) A traditional Manx name, from the Latin name Magnus 'great'.

Margaid f. (MAHR·ged) The Manx form of Margaret.

Mariot f. (MAHR·yot) A Manx nickname for Mary.

Maruna m. (mah·ROO·nuh) From the Old Irish *ma* 'my' + the name Rónán. A pet-name for Rónán that became a name in its own right. Kirk Marown on the Isle of Man is dedicated to Rónán, a traveling Irish saint of the 7th century who is also greatly revered in Brittany. His feast day is January 13.

Mian m. (MII·uhn) A Manx nickname for Matthew.

Michal m. (MIK·uhl) A Manx form of Michael. Another is **Mayl** (MAYL).

Moirrey f. (MOOR·ee) The Manx form of Mary. Nickname: **Mally** (MAH·lee).

Moirrey Malane f. (MOOR·ee ma·LAYN) The Manx form of Mary Madeline.

Mona f. (MOW·nuh) A poetical name for the Isle of Man (and also the name given it by the Romans). Mona Douglas (1898–1987) was a Manx folklorist and language activist.

More f. (MOHR) From the Old Irish name Mór, meaning 'great, tall'.

Mores m. (MAW·ruhs) From the Old Irish name Muirgius: *muir* 'sea' + *gus* 'strength, vigor'.

Murdach m. (MUHR·dah*x*) From the Old Irish *muir* 'sea'.

Myghin f. (MAY·*x*uhn) From the Manx word for 'mercy'.

Nele m. (NAYL) The Manx form of the Irish name Niall, possibly derived from *nél* 'cloud'.

Oran m. (OH·ruhn) From the Old Irish name Odrán 'otter'. Saint Odrán was the charioteer of Saint Patrick. His feast day is February 27.

Orry m. (OH·ree), **Gorry** (GOH·ree) After King Godred I, a Norseman who ruled the Isle of Man as well as parts of Ireland and Scotland from 1079–95. The Milky Way is known in Manx as

Raad Mooar Ree Gorry (The Great Way of King Orry). It is said that when Godred landed on Man, and people asked where he had come from, he pointed toward the stars.

Patric m. (PAHT·reek) The Manx form of Pádraig (Patrick), patron saint of Ireland. Nicknames are **Paden** (PAHD·jeen) and **Paton** (PAHT·uhn).

Payl m. (PAHL) The Manx form of Paul.

Peddyr m. (PE*TH*·uhr) The Manx form of Peter.

Roseen f. (ROH·zeen) From the Irish name Róisín, a diminutive of Rós, which may derive from either the Germanic *hros* 'horse' or the English 'rose'.

Rigard m. (RIG·uhrd) The Manx form of Richard. A popular name.

Robart m. (RAWB·uhrt) The Manx form of Robert. The nickname is **Robyn** (RAWB·uhn).

Sorley m. (SOHR·lee) From the Old Norse *summarliethi*, 'one who goes forth in the summer', that is, a Viking. According to the Norse *Orkneyinga Saga,* Vikings spent autumn and winter on the Isle of Man, raiding the nearby coasts in the spring and summer. This was the name of a 12th-century ruler of 'The Isles', a Gaelic kingdom that included the Isle of Man, Southern Hebrides, and the territory of Argyll in Scotland.

Thomase m. (taw·MAHS) The Manx form of Thomas. A nickname is **Thomlyn** (TAWM·lin).

Urmen m. (OOR·muhn) From an Old Irish name, Érémon. Érémon led the legendary Sons of Mil to Ireland to avenge his uncle Ith, who had been slain by the Tuatha Dé Danann.

Vorgell f. (VOHR·guhl) From the Old Irish name Muirgel: *muir* 'sea' + *gel* 'bright, shining'.

Wilmot m. (WIL·muht) The Manx form of William.

Ysbal f. (IZ·buhl) The Manx form of Isabel.

A CALENDAR OF CELTIC SAINTS

JANUARY

1 Oissíne
4 Fianait
5 Ciar
6 Melan
6 Muadnat
13 Rónán
14 Kentigern
15 Íte
19 Brevalaer
22 Lonán
24 Cadoc
25 Dwynwen
26 Conan
28 Eochaid
28 Meallán
31 Gweltas

FEBRUARY

1 Brígid
3 Caélfind
6 Macha
7 Derrien
7 Meallán
9 Caírech
9 Rónán
9 Teilo
11 Gobnait
12 Riok
14 Conran
15 Berach
17 Girec
18 Lassar
24 Roparzh
27 Odrán

MARCH

1 Dewi
2 Slébíne
3 Gwenole
5 Piran
8 Senán
9 Costentyn
9 Melle
10 Kavan
10 Kado
11 Óengus
17 Pádraig
29 Gladez

APRIL

4 Tigernach
6 Bearchán
6 Neven
7 Goron
8 Tigernán
15 Rúadán
17 Donnan
17 Eochaid
22 Ceallachán
27 Newlyna
29 Endelyon

MAY

1 Bryok
1 Corentyn
1 Oissíne
3 Cairbre
3 Conláed
3 Ewen

MAY (CONT'D)

3 Glewas
8 Odrán
9 Tudi
10 Comgall
16 Brendan
17 Madron
19 Erwan
21 Collen
22 Luíseach
23 Crimthann
24 David
26 Becan

JUNE

3 Brandubh
4 Beryan
4 Breaca
4 Cáemgen
4 Petrock
6 Jarlath
7 Meriadec
9 Colm Cille
10 Margaret
17 Herve
17 Neythen
19 Rivanon
28 Austell

JULY

3 Garmon
3 Kilian
5 Morwenna
6 Nolwenn

JULY (CONT'D)

16 Mac Dara
21 Trifin
23 Seva
24 Declán
28 Samzun
29 Silyen

AUGUST

4 Sithny
11 Blane
16 Arzhel
23 Eogán
26 Edern
30 Rewan
31 Aidan

SEPTEMBER

9 Ciarán
11 Deiniol
11 Glen
12 Ailbe
15 Mirren
21 Mabyn
24 Donan
25 Finnbarr
26 Mawgan
27 Barri
28 Konan
28 Mac Dara
30 Leri

OCTOBER

3 Klervi
6 Arzhur
8 Morgana
9 Cadwaladr
11 Cainnech
13 Comgán
14 Enora
14 Manacca
14 Seleven
16 Ciar
21 Marcán
25 Alor
26 Meallán

NOVEMBER

1 Cadfan
1 Cairbre
3 Jenifry
3 Levenez
3 Malachy
5 Kea
6 Efflam
6 Gwenn
8 Treveur
12 Machonna
13 Bricius
14 Lorcán
15 Malo

NOVEMBER (CONT'D)

16 Govran
18 Kevern
19 Edana
22 Aziliz
23 Colmán
24 Bleuzenn
27 Alan
27 Tangi
28 Heodez
29 Fianait
30 Cryda
30 Tudual

DECEMBER

1 Alar
7 Azenor
8 Budoc
11 Deniel
12 Kaourantin
16 Judikaël
22 Briac
23 Gwenvael
25 Koulm

Many of these saints' names have several different spellings, as well as nicknames. You can find these variants by looking up the name given in this calendar in the index.

INDEX

Miles, 50
Milyan, 97
Mirren, 26
Moira, 49
Móirín, 51
Moirrey, 107
Moirrey Malane, 107
Mona, 51, 70, 107
Montgomery, 26
Mór, 50
Mórag, 27
Morann, 51
More, 107
Moreen, 51
Mores, 107
Morfudd, Morfydd, 70
Morgan, 70
Morgana, Morgane, 85
Morganez, 86
Morgant, 70
Morgelyn, 98
Morna, 27, 51
Morvan, 86
Morvana, 86
Morven, 27
Morvoren, 98
Morvyn, 27
Morwen, 70
Morwenna, 70, 98
Morwennol, 98
Muadhnait, 51
Muadnat, 51
Muir, 27
Muireall, 27
Muireann, 51
Muirín, 51
Muiríol, 51
Muiríos, 51
Muirne, 27, 51
Munro, 27
Murchadh, 27, 52

Murdach, 107
Murdo, 27
Murdoch, 27
Myfanwy, 70
Myfi, Myfina, 70
Myghal, 98
Myghin, 107
Myles, 50
Myrddin, 70
Myrna, 51
Nadelek, 98
Naomhin, 27
Nedeleg, 86
Nele, 107
Nerys, 70
Nessa, 16, 27, 51, 98
Nessie, 16
Nest, Nesta, 70
Neven, 86
Nevena, 86
Nevenez, 86
Nevin, 28
Newlyna, 98
Neythen, 98
Nia, 70
Niall, 28, 52
Niallán, 52
Niam, 52
Niamh, 52
Nicca, 98
Nikolaz, 86
Nolwenn, 86
Nona, 71
Nonita, 71
Nonn, 86
Nonna, 86, 98
Nonnita, 86
Nora, Norah, 52
Noric, Norig, 79
Nuala, 46
Oanez, 86

Odrán, 52
Óengus, 35
Oighrig, 21
Oisín, 52
Oissíne, 52
Olier, 86
Olwen, 71
Oona, Oonagh, 56
Oran, 52, 107
Oregon, 78
Órlaith, 52
Órla, 52
Orry, 107
Oscar, 53
Osla, 28
Ossian, 28
Owain, Owein, 71
Owen, 21
Padan, 28
Paden, 108
Padern, 98
Pádraig, 53
Pádraigin, 53
Padrig, 71, 86
Padriga, 86
Padruig, 28
Padyn, 28
Paol, 86
Paola, 87
Parlan, 28
Parry, 71
Partholon, 28
Pasco, Pascow, 98
Pasgen, 71
Paton, 28, 108
Patric, 108
Patrick, 53, 71, 86
Pawl, 71
Pawly, 98
Payl, 108
Peadair, 28

Silyen, 99
Sim, 29
Simon, 29
Sine, 29, 55
Sinéad, 55
Siobhán, 55
Siobhánín, 55
Síomha, 55
Siôn, 73
Sioned, 73
Sioni, 73
Sionyn, 73
Siôr, 73
Sithny, 99
Siwan, 73
Sláine, 55
Slany, 55
Slébíne, Sléibhín, 55
Soa, 81
Soaic, 81
Somairle, 29
Somerled, 29
Sorcha, 29
Sorley, 108
Sterenn, 87
Stewart, 30
Stiùbhart, 29
Struan, 29
Stuart, 29
Suibhne, 55
Sulgwen, 87
Sulien, 73
Sweeney, 55
Sym, Syme, 29
Talan, 99
Talek, 99
Taliesin, 73
Talwyn, 90
Tamara, 100
Tàmhas, 30
Tamon, 100

Tamsyn, 100
Tanet, 87
Tangi, Tanguy, 87
Tanick, 88
Tanwen, 73
Tara, 55
Taran, 88
Tárlach, 55
Teamhair, 55
Teàrlach, 29
Teca, 100
Tegan, 73
Tegau, 73
Tegeirian, 73
Tegwen, 73
Teilo, 74
Teleri, 74
Tewdwr, 74
Teyrnon, 74
Thomase, 108
Thomlyn, 108
Tiarnach, 56
Tiarnán, 56
Tib, Tibbie, Tibby, 24
Tierney, 56
Tigernach, 56
Tigernán, 56
Tin, 84
Tinic, Tinig, 84
Tòmas, 30
Tomos, 74
Tonan, 80
Torcaill, 30
Torkill, 30
Torquil, 30
Tracy, 56
Treasach, 56
Trefor, 74
Tressa, 100
Trevedic, 100
Treveur, 88

Trifin, 88
Trifine, 88
Tríona, 38
Tristan, 88, 100
Tristana, 88
Trystan, 100
Tudi, 88
Tudor, 74
Tudual, 88
Tudur, 74
Tudy, 88
Tugdual, 88
Turlough, 56
Twm, 74
Tyrone, 56
Uilleam, 30
Uisdean, 30
Una, 30, 56
Urmen, 108
Uther, 100
Vana, 86
Vorgell, 108
Wallace, 30
Walter, 30
Wella, 100
Wilmot, 100, 108
Withell, 100
Wmffre, 74
Wyllow, 100
Wylmet, 100
Yann, 88
Yannick, Yannig, 88
Ygerna, 100
Ysbal, 108
Yvon, 81
Yvona, 81
Zethar, 100

RECOMMENDED READING

Autret, Yvon. 1982. *Les prénoms de Bretagne.* Rennes: Ouest-France.

Bice, Christopher. 1984. *Names for the Cornish.* Redruth: Dyllansow Truarn.

Dixon, Piers. 1973. *Cornish Names.* Probus: P. Dixon.

Dunkling, Leslie. 1978. *Scottish Christian Names: An A-Z of First Names.* London: Johnston and Bacon.

Evans, D. Ellis. 1967. *Gaulish Personal Names: A Study of Some Continental Formations.* Oxford: Clarendon Press.

Gall, Martin J., and James Fife, eds. 1993. *The Celtic Languages.* London: Routledge.

Green, Miranda J. 1992. *Dictionary of Celtic Myth and Legend.* New York: Thames and Hudson.

Gruffudd, Heini. 1980. *Enwau Cymraeg I Blant / Welsh Names for Children.* Talybont, Dyfed: Y Lolfa.

Le Menn, Gwennole. 1990. *Grand choix de prénoms bretons.* Spezed: Coop Breizh.

MacAulay, Donald, ed. *The Celtic Languages.* 1992. Cambridge: Cambridge University Press.

MacLysaght, Edward. 1991. *The Surnames of Ireland.* 6th ed. Dublin: Irish Academic Press.

Ó Corráin, Donnchadh, and Fidelma Maguire. 1990. *Irish Names.* 2nd ed. Dublin: Lilliput Press.

Rees, Alwyn and Brinley Rees. 1961. *Celtic Heritage: Ancient Tradition in Ireland and Wales.* London: Thames and Hudson.

Rosenkrantz, Linda, and Pamela Redmond Satran. 1992. *Beyond Shannon and Sean: An Enlightened Guide to Irish Baby Naming.* New York: St. Martin's Press.